LUTHERAN HIGH SCHOOL RELIGION SERIES T.M.

For God So Loved...

A Study of the Gospel of John

Teachers Guide for Grade 9

Prepared by: David Widenhofer

Edited by Board for Parish Services Staff
Editor: Jane L. Fryar
Editorial Secretary: Glenna Miesner

Publishing House
St. Louis

Write to Library for the Blind, 1333 S. Kirkwood Road, St. Louis, MO 63122-7295 to obtain "For God So Loved . . ." (Teachers Guide) in Braille or sightsaving print for the visually impaired.

Unless otherwise stated, the Scripture quotations in this publication are from The Holy Bible: NEW INTERNATIONAL VERSION, copyright c 1978 by the International Bible Society. Used by permission of Zondervan Bible Publishers.

Bible quotations marked RSV are from the Revised Standard Version of the Bible, copyrighted 1946, 1952, c 1971, 1973 by the Division of Christian Education of the National Council of the Churches of Christ in the U.S.A., and are used by permission.

Bible quotations marked TEV are from the Good News Bible, the Bible in TODAY'S ENGLISH VERSION. Copyright American Bible Society 1966, 1971, 1976. Used by permission.

Scripture quotations marked NASB are from the NEW AMERICAN STANDARD BIBLE, c The Lockman Foundation 1960, 1962, 1963, 1968, 1971, 1972, 1973, 1975, and are used by permission.

Copyright 1986 Concordia Publishing House
3558 S. Jefferson Avenue,
St. Louis, MO 63118-3968
Manufactured in the United States of America

All rights reserved. No part of this publication may be reproduced, stored in a retrieval system, or transmitted, in any form or by any means, electronic, mechanical, photocopying, recording, or otherwise, without the prior written permission of Concordia Publishing House.

Contents

To the Teacher	4

Unit 1: Fly Like An Eagle

1 The Gospel in a Gospel [Matthew, Mark, Luke, and John]	6
2 On Eagle's Wings [John]	7
3 Law and Gospel in a Gospel [Rom. 5--6; Galatians]	10
4 Key Words in John [John 1--21]	11
5 The Gospel According to Me (Part 1) [John 1--21]	13
6 The Gospel According to Me (Part 2) [John 1--21]	14
7 Jesus--the Logos of God [John 1:1-18]	15
8 Jesus--the Lamb of God [John 1:19-51]	16
9 Jesus' First Sign [John 2:1-11]	18
10 Jesus--the Temple of God [John 2:12-24]	20
11 Concluding Activities for Unit 1 [John 1--2]	22

Unit 2: Jesus--the Way, the Truth, the Life

12 Born Again! [John 3:1-21]	24
13 The Light of His Love [John 3:1-21]	26
14 Quenching Your Thirst [John 4:1-26]	28
15 Sharing the Living Water [John 4:1-42]	30
16 I Am the Bread of Life (Part 1) [John 6:1-15 and 25-69]	31
17 I Am the Bread of Life (Part 2) [John 6:1-15 and 25-69]	33
18 A Growing Storm of Controversy [John 7:1-52]	35
19 Authority to Forgive Sins [John 8:1-11]	37
20 Following the Light of Jesus [John 8:12-30]	38
21 Freedom! [John 8:31-59]	40
22 Now I See! [John 9]	42
23 I Am the Good Shepherd [John 10]	44
24 The Resurrection Connection [John 11:1-42]	46
25 Concluding Activities for Unit 2 [John 3--11]	48

Unit 3: Bearing Much Fruit

26 Anointed for the Mission [John 11:42--12:11]	49
27 Glorify Your Name! [John 12:12-50]	51
28 The Sign of a Servant [John 13:1-17; Matt. 20:20-28]	53
29 Is It I, Lord? [John 13:18-30]	55
30 Love One Another [John 13:31-38]	57
31 Jesus, the Way to the Father [John 14:1-14]	59
32 The Promise of the Spirit [John 14:15-31; 16:5-16]	61
33 Abiding in Christ [John 15:1-17]	63
34 Standing Against the World [John 15:18-27]	65
35 Jesus Prays for His People (Part 1) [John 17]	67
36 Jesus Prays for His People (Part 2) [John 17]	68
37 Concluding Activities for Unit 3 [John 11--17]	70

Unit 4: Crucified and Risen

38 Jesus Died for Me! (Part 1) [John 18--21]	71
39 Jesus Died for Me! (Part 2) [John 18--21]	72
40 The Cup of God's Wrath [John 18:1-11]	73
41 On Trial [John 18:12--19:16]	74
42 Are You Sure? [John 20]	76
43 Feed My Lambs [John 21]	77
44 Fly Like an Eagle [John 1--21]	79
45 Concluding Activities [John 1--21]	80

To the Teacher

"For God So Loved . . .," designed for ninth grade students, provides an overview of John's gospel with particular emphasis on Jesus' teachings as found in this gospel. Students will practice using various Bible study tools as they study the gospel. Special attention is also given to key words and themes that recur throughout the book.

This course may be taught in grade 10 or (with adaptation) in grade 11 or 12.

"For God So Loved . . ." is a 45 session course, providing resources for one quarter. We recommend class five days per week. However, if your class meets less often, you might (a) extend the material in this course over a longer period of time, (b) assign certain sessions to individuals or small groups for reports in class, or (c) select sessions or units in accordance with class periods available.

THE LUTHERAN HIGH SCHOOL RELIGION SERIES

This is one of 12 courses for Lutheran high schools. The courses have been designed to permit use with a variety of scheduling programs. Four courses contain 90 sessions each and provide materials for five sessions per week for one semester. Each of the other eight courses contains 45 sessions, and is designed for one quarter (half a semester).

Following are the topics of the 12 courses:

Grade 9
Fitting In: Relationships with God and Others (45 sessions)
"For God So Loved . . .": A Study of the Gospel of John (45 sessions)
God's Old Testament People (90 sessions)

Grade 10
New Testament history--including early church history (90 sessions)
The church in Paul's epistles (45 sessions)
Christian ethics (45 sessions)

Grade 11
Christian doctrine (90 sessions)
Later church history: Luther and the Reformation; Lutheranism (45 sessions)
Christian and non-Christian religions and cults (45 sessions)

Grade 12
Personal Christian living (90 sessions)
Engagement and marriage (45 sessions)
The general epistles and Revelation (45 sessions)

This design was prepared after a survey of all high schools affiliated with Association for Lutheran Secondary Schools and after extensive conversations with high-school and college teachers. Thus, it reflects both current practices and theory. The Parish Services staff wishes to express a special word of thanks to the ALSS administrators for their cooperation and assistance.

While any course assumes a certain background and maturity of the students, each course can stand alone--a previous course in this series is not an absolute prerequisite. The Student Books contain no grade-level designations; therefore courses can be adapted to other grade levels.

MATERIALS

In addition to this guide, you will need a copy of the accompanying Student Book and a Bible. (This course generally quotes the New International Version of the Bible. We recommend that you select a translation commonly used in the congregations of your students.)

The students will need a copy of the Student Book and a Bible. Many lessons assume that students have access to other resources as well. These include Bible commentaries, dictionaries, concordances, topical Bible handbooks, and maps.

USING THIS GUIDE

Some sessions suggest more activities than can be accomplished in one period. Be selective. You know your students. Use the activities and materials that will be of most value to them.

LAW AND GOSPEL

The plans in this guide help you structure sessions so that students see both Law and Gospel. You will want the Holy Spirit to work in them as they hear God's words of accusation, forgiveness, and guidance. As you begin to plan the course, you might reread <u>The Proper Distinction Between Law and Gospel</u> by C. F. W. Walther. This is good reading for all who work with youth, especially teachers.

Once (**John 12:20-21**) some Greeks came to Philip and said, **"Sir, we would like to see Jesus."** Your basic goal as you teach each day should be to bring students to "see Jesus." Confront them with their spiritual needs; then lead them to see Jesus their Savior as the Answer to those needs. Let His love permeate all relationships in your classroom as you grow together in grace by the Spirit's power. Set this as your primary goal, and let all other objectives grow within this goal.

We invite you to write the editors about "For God So Loved . . ." Share the joys and frustrations you experienced as you taught this course, offer suggestions for other courses, etc. Please send your comments to:

Editorial Services Unit
Board for Parish Services
The Lutheran Church--Missouri Synod
1333 South Kirkwood Road
St. Louis, MO 63122-7295

A NOTE FROM THE AUTHOR

The Gospel of John is an appropriate place to begin a study of the New Testament. It contains many of Jesus' great teachings and recurring themes.

Making a Biblical book come alive for teenagers is no easy task! It demands patience, creativity, persistence, prayer, and a teacher who models the message. Our temptation is always to overindulge in "teacher talk" and cognitive exercises. Yet, ideally, the theology class can model the methods of Jesus--read and listen, reflect, ask, consider, and believe!

Many young people perceive Christianity to involve no more than prescribed behavior based on a belief in God. The call to faith and forgiveness are often ignored or missed. Therefore a study of the fourth gospel must be more than an academic activity to learn facts about the life of Jesus. John's purpose is that the reader more firmly trust and believe in Jesus Christ as Lord and Savior. The content and methods of this course have been prepared to enable that to take place--both in the hearts of the students and in the heart of the teacher.

Unit 1: Fly Like an Eagle

This unit overviews the entire gospel John wrote and compares it with the synoptic gospels, accenting similarities and differences. It rehearses some of the most basic principles of Biblical interpretation and encourages students to apply their personal Bible reading to their daily lives.

PLANNING THE UNIT

Note that this course makes frequent reference to student notebooks. Think about how you want students to organize their notebooks and what things you will expect them to include. You may want to skim through the material in this guide as you make your decisions.

Session 1: The Gospel in a Gospel

BIBLE BASIS: Matthew, Mark, Luke, John

CENTRAL TRUTH

The gospel accounts of the New Testament present four distinctive pictures of the one Savior, Jesus Christ. Their common purpose is to proclaim the truth about God's love for sinners. The writers, inspired by the Holy Spirit, intend their readers to go beyond intellectual assent to the facts about Jesus. They wrote that we **"may believe that Jesus is the Christ, the Son of God, and that by believing, [we] may have life in His name"** (John 20:31).

OBJECTIVES

That the students will:
1. Explain the general differences between the synoptic gospels and the gospel of John
2. Recognize the central purpose of the gospels, namely to elicit faith as the Spirit works through His Word
3. Reaffirm their faith in Jesus as the Savior verbally to others in the class

BACKGROUND

Bible students for centuries have studied the four gospel accounts, fascinated by the unique picture of the Savior painted by each of the four inspired writers. Even when recording the same event in the life of Christ, each gospel reveals a different facet of Jesus' compassion or a new aspect of God's truth.

As you work through today's lesson with your students, you will explore briefly what has come to be called the synoptic question: What is the relationship between the first three gospels to one another and to John's account? As you prepare, you may want to read the introductory materials for each of the four gospels from the Concordia Self-Study Commentary. You should also consult other references mentioned in the bibliography at the back of this guide.

Of course, a merely cognitive discussion of the relationship of the gospel accounts to one another would be unfaithful to the purpose for which the writers wrote. These accounts, though biographical, go beyond biography. The gospel writers proclaimed the Gospel as they retold the life story of Jesus the Messiah. Jesus said, **"I have come that they may have life, and have it to the full"** (John 10:10). John himself tells us of his overriding concern: **"Jesus did many other miraculous signs in the presence of His disciples, which are not recorded in this book. But these are written that you may believe that Jesus is the Christ, the Son of God, and that by believing you may have life in His name"** (20:30-31).

The goal for this class session must be that each student confront the claims of Jesus as the only Savior of the world. For some students, this may be new. For others, the call to repentance and faith will be a call for renewal. But without this kerygmatic dimension, the theology class loses the life-giving potential unique to Christian education. **Pray** that each student today will hear the Gospel in the gospels.

SEARCHING THE SCRIPTURES
(Objective 1)

To help your students understand the differing viewpoints of the gospel writers, begin with a writing exercise similar to that described in the introduction for this session in the Student Book. A number of possibilities exist:

a. Have each student write a paragraph describing a recent event in which they all took part--a football game, a play, a concert, etc.

b. Stage an event in class. For example, you might ask an older student or another teacher to come into the classroom just as the class period starts. This person should begin arguing heatedly with you. Then explain what you have done and ask the students to write a description of the event.

c. Arrange several days before this class session to have several of your students photograph a particular scene or person that will be familiar to your class. If some of the photographers are skillful with a camera and some not so artistic, all the better. The time of day, the type of camera, the kinds of lenses used, and the angle at which the photos are taken will all effect the outcome.

Whichever option you choose, have several students read what they have written. Spend enough time with the activity so that the students recognize that each of us approaches any given experience from a unique viewpoint and that our unique viewpoint determines what parts of an experience we will highlight when we tell about it.

WHAT'S THE DIFFERENCE? (Objectives 1 and 2)

Work through the exercises together in class. Students will need both their Bibles and the chart found in the back of the Student Book.

TO SEE TOGETHER (Objectives 2 and 3)

Focus especially on the second part of this section.

Call attention to the key words listed on the page. Explain your procedure for dealing with these in each unit. Students should record definitions in one format or another for the key words for the course.

Close the class period by presenting your purpose for the course, your goals, and any classroom procedures you find pertinent. Explain the class notebook you expect each student to keep and give the students details as to what things they should include and the format you want them to use.

OPTIONAL ACTIVITIES

Assign as homework any questions from the Student Book you have not covered in class. The optional activities may be assigned or offered as extra credit projects to those students who need to be challenged.

Session 2: On Eagle's Wings

BIBLE BASIS: The Book of John

CENTRAL TRUTH

John wrote to proclaim the truth that Jesus is the Christ, the Son of God, and that faith in Him will yield life in all its fullness. Insight into John's purpose, style, perspective, and special themes enhances the readers' understanding of God's truth.

OBJECTIVES

That the students will:

1. Write a brief paper explaining John's personal background and relationship with Jesus

2. Recognize the theological nature of John's gospel as compared with the synoptics and understand the reason for this

3. Grow in their own personal faith relationship with Jesus as true God, true man--their Savior

BACKGROUND

This lesson has been designed to give students the necessary background for a careful study of John's gospel. They will use this information and insight throughout the rest of the course. You will want to help your students understand that when Christians interpret the Scriptures, we begin first by probing the meaning the text held for its original audience. To understand John's meaning, we need to keep in mind the motifs he uses and his purposeful selection of material. Guided by the Holy Spirit, the author records events from Christ's life and teachings from His ministry to accomplish God's purposes in the hearts of the gospel's readers.

Scholars have debated the identity of the author, "the disciple whom Jesus loved." While various suggestions have been made, the general consensus and traditional view is that John the apostle, one of the "Sons of Thunder," wrote the fourth gospel.

As an eyewitness, John records Jesus' ministry with a primary focus on the ministry in Jerusalem. Unlike the synoptics, which deal largely with the Lord's Galilean ministry, John begins already in the second chapter to explain Jesus' relationship with the Jewish temple leaders. This gospel recounts the heated differences that surfaced when Jesus proclaimed Himself the Christ, the fulfillment of the Old Testament Messianic prophesies. The Pharisees and Sadducees, ordinarily theological antagonists, join forces to oppose Jesus' claims. Throughout the book, these religious leaders are grouped together and referred to as "the Jews."

Already in **John 7:32** Jesus' religious opponents seek His arrest and on more than one occasion the Savior escapes a murderous mob that threatens to kill Him.

Besides presenting the Lord's claims to the title Messiah, John wrote to counter the gnostic heresy. By the time John wrote his gospel (A.D. 90--100), Christianity had been established in the Mediterranean world. The apostles and other missionaries had taken the Gospel message to every major city and country.

By mixing a little truth with many of his own lies, Satan succeeded in spreading drastic error throughout much of this infant church. The gnostic heresy held that deity could not have been contained in real human flesh. Jesus, therefore, must have been some kind of ghost without real flesh and blood. Docetism (from the Greek word dokein--to seem) concluded that Jesus only seemed to be human.

John, Colossians, and other New Testament books address this error in the strongest terms. (See especially **2 John.**) William Barclay summarizes the implications of the heresy succinctly: "Gnostic beliefs at one and the same time destroyed the real godhead and the real manhood of Jesus." (See Barclay's The Gospel of John, vol. 1.)

Several texts in John's gospel reflect the apostle's confrontation with gnosticism. As you prepare to teach, you will want to read **John 1:1-5; 2:15; 4:6, 31; 11:33-38; 19:28;** and the texts listed in the Student Book.

GETTING INTO THE LESSON
Lead a brief discussion about eagles and possible reasons for the selection of this symbol to represent the gospel of John. John records various discourses of the Savior that soar to the heights of theological truth. John teaches us about the lofty nature of the Son of God. He stresses the meaning of events, rather than the facts of particular events in and of themselves.

A SON OF THUNDER (Objective 1)
Lead the class through this section. You may want to let the students work with a partner as they develop their character sketches of the apostle.

A PORTRAIT OF THE SAVIOR (Objectives 2 and 3)
Most students should have little trouble completing the first part of this section on their own. If time does not permit a complete discussion of all parts of the lesson in class,

assign it as homework.

The last paragraph deals with information about John's first readers. You may wish to share with taken from the **Background** section of this guide.

If you prefer that your students begin to learn basic research skills, assign this part of the lesson for student research. If you do this, though, be sure to provide adequate research tools. Also be sure to help those students who are unfamiliar with research techniques. You might require that the students record their findings in their notebooks or that they write a one- to two-page paper toy our students notes on gnosticism report.

IMPORTANT QUESTIONS (Objective 3)

The last section of the Student Book deserves attention in class. Nearly all of today's cults confuse the nature of Christ in one way or another. You may want to share the chart below with your students. As you do, stress the implications for our faith in Jesus if He were not true God and if He were not true man.

Jesus/Christ

Church	Beliefs	Source
Christian	True God and true man; eternal; the only Savior	Bible only
Pseudo-Christian, e.g., Latter Day Saints	Born as a normal child of man and woman or God and woman. We can become what He was.	Bible and other "revelations"
Jehovah's Witnesses	Born as a normal man, He led an exemplary life.	Bible and human reason
Eastern religions, such as Hinduism	One of many expressions of God. Jesus and Christ are separate. Jesus discovered His "Christ-nature"; we, too, possess this and must discover it.	Tradition
Other Eastern religions	Every age has its "divine master" or "God walking on earth"; Jesus was the one for His age.	Tradition
New Age Religion	Combines elements of all the above. Each person is God and must realize it.	Secular humanism; all "sacred literature;" traditions; plus "new consciousness"

Session 3: Law and Gospel in a Gospel

BIBLE BASIS: Rom. 5--8; Galatians 1--6

CENTRAL TRUTH

Scripture can be correctly interpreted only as one recognizes and applies Law and Gospel in it. The central message of Scripture is that God has provided a solution to the dreadful dilemma of human sin: In grace, He sent His only Son Jesus to die for all. By trusting this Good News, we share in the joy and love of God, receive His forgiveness, claim the sure hope of everlasting life, and receive power to live as God's redeemed children.

OBJECTIVES

That the students will:

1. Use Law and Gospel as they read and apply Scripture to their personal lives and as they study the **Book of John** in this course
2. Identify the three uses of the Law and see how these have been drawn from Scripture
3. Understand the difference between grace and the human idea of salvation based on personal merit or effort
4. Use the power of God's love to live more holy lives

BACKGROUND

For the most part, our world operates according to a system of law. Society could not exist without law and order. We come to count on the law, on its logic and predictability, to stabilize our lives.

The idea of grace, of salvation and eternal life given to us by God as a free gift, runs counter to our natural human sense of how things should be. Unregenerate sinners feel threatened by it. Grace lies beyond our control. The idea that we can do nothing to earn God's love, that He loves us with infinite love no matter what, that He loves us with eternal love regardless of what we've done or been and regardless of what we could ever do or be--that kind of love is an affront to our pride. We struggle to grasp at least some credit for our own salvation.

Law feels more comfortable. We can see the logic in a system of reward-and-punishment. A Law orientation allows us to control our own destiny. Law, works, rules, pride, guilt--even though such a system makes us feel uncomfortable at times, our flesh prefers that we be masters of our fate, the captains of our own souls.

Even after we come to recognize our own inability to keep God's law and even after we come to see our need for Jesus' atoning work on our behalf, we are often tempted to put ourselves back under that curse from which Christ has redeemed us. How easily and subtly we distort grace and twist the Gospel into Law. Even after we come to faith, our flesh tries so desperately to justify our sin somehow. It struggles so hard to earn the Father's love.

"Jesus loves me, so I'd better shape up."

"How many times can God forgive me for this same sin?"

"If God forgives anyway, I may as well live it up!"

Despair and arrogance. How often we see these attitudes in ourselves and in our students! Probably much oftener than we would care to admit. These distortions of God's grace keep us from living the rich, full lives the Father intends for His children.

So, then, today's lesson involves more than an academic exercise in recognizing Law and Gospel in particular pericopes of Scripture. Rather, we want to help our students recognize the trap of legalism. We want them to be able to use the Law as God has intended. And we want them to see the power, the dynamite of the Gospel (**Rom. 1:16**), that can transform their lives into an exciting adventure, into lives of peace and joy in the Lord Jesus.

Before you teach this lesson, we

recommend you review C. F. W. Walther's A Proper Distinction Between Law and Gospel. You might also find it helpful to reread article 4 of the Apology of the Augsburg Confession.

BAD NEWS/GOOD NEWS (Objectives 1 and 2)

Use the cartoon strip and the introduction beneath it to help your students begin thinking about the concepts of Law and Gospel. Then read the paragraphs that give a preliminary definition of each.

Have the class read **Rom. 7:7-12**. Stress the idea that the Law is, in and of itself, good. But because we are sinful, the Law incites us to rebellion. Have the class think of examples of times people do things just because they have been told not to do them. (It may be easier if they first think of times little children act in this way. Then have them give examples from their own lives and the lives of adults.)

LAW BREAKERS (Objective 2)

This part of the lesson should lead the students to identify the three uses of the Law from Scripture. The Law was given by God to help prevent gross outbreaks of sin in society, to show people their sin and their need for the Savior, and as a guide to Christians in knowing how they can live happily as God's sanctified children. The Law existed before the Ten Commandments were given on Mt. Sinai because God wrote His law in human hearts. Even though the Law has been distorted by sin, it has never been erased.

As the class brainstorms words to describe the Law, write them on a chalkboard or a large piece of poster paper. Keep the list on display. You will use it later in the period.

NOT GUILTY!?! (Objective 3)

Have someone read the story that appears at the beginning of this section. Depending on the background of your students, you may wish to review such words as justification, salvation, redemption, and atonement at this point as well.

Then talk about grace and its meaning. As an alternative to having students find and read definitions of grace in class, you might assign a word study to be completed before the next class session. Ask each student to consult three or four sources and then summarize their findings in writing, perhaps in their notebooks.

GOOD NEWS (Objectives 3 and 4)

1. Have the class read the parable and then tell it to one another, putting it into a contemporary setting and telling it in contemporary language. Then discuss the questions from the Student Book.

2. If time does not permit you to do this section in class, it could be assigned as homework.

3. Make a list of words next to the list you brainstormed earlier. Let students look through some of Paul's epistles for further ideas. Contrast the two lists. Ask, **Do you think you live most of your time under the Law or under grace? Explain.**

Use texts such as **2 Cor. 5:15-17** and **Rom. 6:8-11** to help them see the difference.

4. Have the students write the personalized version of this verse in their class notebooks.

Encourage the students to be specific and precise as they answer the last question for themselves. Be sure to discuss self-image as well as attitudes and conduct. Also be sure this discussion does not become subtly Law oriented.

Session 4: Key Words in John

BIBLE BASIS: John 1—21

CENTRAL TRUTH

Jesus came to earth to live and die for us so that we could receive abundant and eternal life. We receive this life by God's grace through faith in the Savior.

OBJECTIVES

That the students will:
1. Recognize some key words that

recur throughout the Gospel of John

2. Develop preliminary definitions for some of John's key words as an aid to understanding the concepts behind them when they read various pericopes throughout the course

3. Rely upon God's grace to empower them to live the abundant life about which John wrote

BACKGROUND

<u>What do I really believe?</u>
<u>What **is** true, after all?</u>
<u>How can I be happy?</u>
<u>What things combine to give a person a successful, fulfilled life?</u>

As young people evaluate life-styles, as they make moral decisions and vocational choices, as they think about their relationships with other people, and as they struggle with the questions involved in making the Christian faith their own, they look for absolutes, for foundations on which they can rely.

John's gospel speaks eloquently to the questions of meaning and truth our students face. Today's lesson introduces several key words from John's gospel. These words recur as John addresses many of the questions adolescents find most bothersome.

John drops these key words one by one like pebbles into the stream of his narrative. As he repeats each word again and again, its meaning expands in ever-widening ripples of meaning and implication. As you teach today, help your students become aware of the meaning of some of the words that are key to a correct understanding of John's gospel. Before you teach, pray that the Holy Spirit will apply the concepts you will discuss to the practical problems and questions your students face in their everyday lives.

GETTING INTO THE LESSON

Give students a few minutes to design the ads described in the Student Book introduction. You may want to bring several magazine ads to class—ads that use the one-word approach suggested in the Student Book directions.

The point of the exercise is that some words carry with them powerful connotations. These words have the ability to evoke intense feelings and images. Several paragraphs would ordinarily be required to produce the same effect.

The class discussed two "high impact" words for Christians last time—Law and Gospel. Tell the students that today you will explore several "high impact" words John uses in his gospel.

SIGNPOSTS TO LIFE (Objectives 2 and 3)

As a change of pace you may wish to let the students work with partners to complete this section of the lesson. When all have finished, discuss their findings—especially the definitions they wrote.

1. The <u>Concordia Self-Study Commentary</u> notes that the **signs** John records were "wondrous acts which point beyond themselves, from the gift to the Giver." Jesus' **signs** pointed to His authority as the Messiah, the Son of God.

2. Saving faith involves knowing, accepting, and trusting God's plan of salvation by grace through faith for the sake of the Lord Jesus. Mere intellectual assent is worthless, as James points out in the reference listed in the Student Book.

If faith comes as a gift from God as He works through His Word, we need to find/make time to spend in that Word daily.

Talk with your students about their daily Bible reading plan/schedule. Help those who have no such devotional plan to develop one. The length of the Scripture portion matters less than does the consistency and spiritual discipline of such a plan. You may want to require that a part of the students' class notebooks includes brief notes and comments about each of their daily devotional readings during the remainder of this quarter.

As students discuss the last question in this section, have them read **Rom. 6:23**. Ask them to note the verb tense. "The wages of sin <u>is</u> death/the gift of God <u>is</u> eternal life." When do we receive eternal life?

If time permits, have someone use a good Bible dictionary to find the meaning of the word **life**. Compare the dictionary definition with the one the students formulated. Combine the best points from all the definitions to come up with a class definition. Write it on the chalkboard and ask the students to copy it into their notebooks.

THE HOUR OF GLORY (Objectives 1, 2, and 3)

The deeper theological meaning of **time (hour)** may be difficult for some students. God's plan for securing our salvation had its own special timetable. The death of the Savior, the Son of God, did not happen accidentally or simply as a result of human will. The omnipotent, omniscient God directed the flow of history toward the fulfillment of His ancient Messianic promises. Jesus' **hour** came as the Passover lambs were slaughtered on the temple altar and as the Roman soldiers drove the spikes into His hands and hoisted the cross into an upright position on Calvary. Throughout most of John's gospel we anticipate this **hour (time)**, the turning point of all human history.

(**Note:** Remind students that you will examine their notebooks after the next class period.)

Session 5: The Gospel According to Me (Part 1)

BIBLE BASIS: John 1—21

CENTRAL TRUTH

Each of the four gospel accounts presents a portrait of Christ. As we learn to know His love through His Word, our lives become a living portrait of our Savior. Empowered by His grace, we reflect His image in our thoughts, attitudes, words, and actions.

OBJECTIVES

That the students will:
1. Organize and write a personal portrait of Christ drawn from facts recorded in the four gospel accounts
2. Identify the many and varied ways God has brought and continues to bring His good news into their lives and thank God for them
3. Ask God to release His power, love, and forgiveness into a problem situation in their lives

BACKGROUND

During this session and the next, you and the students will work together to apply the power of the Gospel to the personal experiences you each face. No specific Bible portions will be assigned. Rather, the lessons' central activities involve having the students organize a personal gospel account.

This activity provides an opportunity for group sharing and teamwork. You may opt to have each individual student complete the assignment. However, a small group approach will give the students a chance to witness to one another and to practice group problem solving skills. Decide which approach will be most beneficial for your particular students.

Select groups of three to five students to work together on the project. Balance each group as much as possible, taking into account the ability, creativity, and personality of each individual.

Designate one student as team captain and another as author of the final product. This student will be responsible for actually turning in the completed assignment on the day you designate it due.

It will also be helpful for the students if you prepare a sample before class. Include the specific components you want included in the final project. Be sure each student receives a copy of this format. Allow room on the page for students to write. Not all students will have as much Biblical information at their command as will others. Every student, though, will know something about Jesus. Each student's faith and perspective will be different. Class members can learn much from one another if you encourage a classroom atmosphere conducive to such mutual sharing.

Time will probably not permit the students to finish all the activities in class even if you use two class periods. Look over the Student Book directions for both sessions 5 and 6. Then decide which you would like the students to complete in class, which you will assign as homework, and which you will offer as optional extra credit assignments. Base your decision on the needs of the students in this particular class during this particular quarter.

THE GOSPEL ACCORDING TO ME (Objectives 1, 2, and 3)

Begin by discussing the portraits of Christ found in the Student Book. Take about five minutes to share the students responses to the two portraits. What ideas or emotions are presented in each? Does either picture portray Jesus as they understand Him to be? Why do they like (or dislike) each portrait?

Paul's words from **2 Cor. 3:17-18** underscore the truth that we become more and more like Jesus the better we come to know Him.

Then move into the project described in the Student Book. See the comments in session 6 of this guide for more details.

Session 6: The Gospel According to Me (Part 2)

BIBLE BASIS: John 1--21

CENTRAL TRUTH
See session 5.

OBJECTIVES
See session 5.

BACKGROUND
See session 5.

GETTING INTO THE LESSON
Briefly review the assignment you gave during session 5. Be sure each group/individual understands what you expect.

You may want to use a three-part outline as you review. All the papers the class develops should have:
  A. An introduction
  B. A list of seven events from Jesus' life and an explanation beneath each event of why that event has been included in the paper
  C. A conclusion

Encourage students to select their own titles. Each group may also want to produce a cover for the finished product. Be sure each student's name appears on the appropriate group project.

As the students work, be ready to give help as needed. Encourage the students to remain "on-task" and to divide the work fairly.

THE POWER OF THE GOSPEL (Objectives 1 and 2)

It will probably help students if you provide an example for each of the two paragraphs you ask them to write. Select a problem in which sin is the root cause. Then let the students model their responses after yours. (You may want to excuse the authors of the "Gospel According to Me" project from writing these paragraphs.)

Be aware that some students could feel threatened by this assignment. Depending on how much members of the class trust you and one another, they may reveal some intensely personal difficulties. Rather than grading the paragraphs, set aside some time to write personal notes to the students about what they have written. Also set aside some time to pray for each individual student as you read his/her paper.

ROMANS 5:6-11 (Objective 3)

Use this Bible reading as a summary for sessions 5 and 6. Ask a student to read it aloud. Be sure the students understand its message. You may wish to assign parts of it as memory work.

Session 7: Jesus--the Logos of God

BIBLE BASIS: John 1:1-18

CENTRAL TRUTH

Jesus Christ, true God and true Man, came as God's final Word to sinners. He reveals God's glory and His grace to us. We need no longer grope in the darkness of our sin because Jesus, the Light, shows us what God is really like and how we may have a personal relationship with Him.

OBJECTIVES

That the students will:
1. Tell why John began his gospel with the prolog he used
2. Explain key terms in John's prolog, such as logos, light, life, grace, and truth
3. Trust more deeply in Jesus, God's Son, who revealed to us what God is like

BACKGROUND

The prolog with which John begins his gospel stands as one of the most unique portions of the New Testament. In so few words John presents truth after truth--truths too deep to be fully comprehended by finite human minds.

The theological nature of John's gospel becomes evident even from his opening verse. Jesus is the Word of God. He is God incarnate. He is the image of the invisible God. He shows us the fullness of the Father's love. To know Jesus is to know the Father. Apart from Jesus, we experience only death and darkness. To live in Jesus means to receive both light and life from Him by His abundant grace.

It lies well beyond the scope of this guide to provide a complete commentary on each point of the text you might choose to stress with your students. We strongly recommend you consult several Bible commentaries, perhaps including Lenski's <u>The Interpretation of St. John's Gospel</u> (pp. 25--99), before you teach.

GETTING INTO THE LESSON (Objective 1)

Read the introductory materials from the Student Book. Discuss ways we communicate without using any words at all. Then talk about single words that carry great power, words that are especially "charged" emotionally. Racial slurs, for example, carry powerful negative connotations. Words like <u>home, brother, peace,</u> and <u>love</u> carry powerful positive meanings for many people.

Clarify John's concern for communicating a correct and full picture of the Savior to people from different cultural backgrounds--Jews and Greeks.

IN THE BEGINNING . . . (Objectives 2 and 3)

1. Let the students work through this section on their own. Then discuss the lists they have compiled. You may want to put a complete list on the chalkboard for students to copy in their notebooks. The point of this exercise is to give the class a comprehensive overview of John's prolog. In doing so, they should discover some of the richness of John's picture of Christ.

2. To save time, have small groups of students each find one of the references, read it to the class, and summarize what the verse says about the power of God's Word.

WHAT KIND OF GOD DO WE SERVE? (Objective 3)

Explain the terms <u>atheist</u>, <u>agnostic</u>, and <u>deist</u>. As you discuss John's possible response to each, challenge students to find specific verses from the text to support their opinions. Be sure to point out that none of these theories are new. Down through the ages, human sinfulness has led people to deny responsibility to God for their actions. Scripture never attempts to prove God's existence. Yet the entire Scripture portrays God as Almighty, as Creator, as omniscient, omnipresent, and as the One to whom we must someday give an account of our lives.

The passages listed in the last part of this session emphasize Jesus as the world's Creator and Preserver, as being full of the glory of God, as having purified us from our sins, and as showing us what God's loving heart is really like.

If your students need help in developing their writing skills, you could use the paragraph writing exercise as an opportunity to review topic sentences, logic, and progression in writing. Work together in class on a paragraph that will summarize the main ideas of each of the four passages listed. This will lead quite naturally into the one-page paper that is suggested as homework in the next section of the lesson.

TO WRAP IT UP (Objectives 2 and 3)

The directions in the Student Book should be self-explanatory. Encourage the students to use Bible dictionaries and concordances to do some research before they begin writing. Have them use scratch paper to jot down the various ideas they come across and think would like to use. Then they should think of how the ideas fit together. After organizing their thoughts into two or three main groups, they are to write one paragraph to explain each main idea.

Unless your students have done extensive writing before this time, you will probably need to provide a good deal of support, encouragement, and guidance as they work. Think of the assignment as a way to help the class sharpen their thinking and analyzing skills as well as their writing abilities.

Finally, don't forget to challenge the students to personalize their paper. Stress should lie mainly on what the truth means to me.

Rather than giving the papers letter grades, you may want to make personal comments on each paper. Give the individual students hints as to how they can improve their paper and ask for a rewrite. Then grade the final result.

Reading assignment for the next session: **John 1:19-51**

Session 8: Jesus--the Lamb of God

BIBLE BASIS: John 1:19-51

CENTRAL TRUTH

Jesus Christ is the Lamb of God, sent to earth to redeem people from their sins. He died to take away the sin of the world.

OBJECTIVES

That the students will:
1. Describe the relationship between John the Baptizer and Jesus
2. Identify some of the Biblical implications of Jesus' title "Lamb of God"
3. Testify to one another about what it means that Jesus is the Lamb of God slain for their redemption

BACKGROUND

John the Baptizer occupies a unique place in salvation history. In many ways, he follows in the footsteps of the Old Testament prophets. He picks up their message: Repent!

Yet John proclaimed not so much the requirements of the Old Covenant as the coming of the New. Jesus identifies John as "Elijah," the forerunner of Messiah. (See **Mal. 4:5** and **Matt. 11:14**.) Perhaps surprisingly, none of the four gospel writers records a single miracle performed by John. Rather, his role as God's messenger remains paramount throughout his ministry.

One characteristic of that ministry is undeniable: John spoke with authority. Because he did so with such zeal, he clashed frequently with the religious leaders of his day. As they questioned his right to preach and to baptize, John repeatedly and emphatically disavowed any claim to being the Messiah himself. Rather, he pointed out his preparatory role. Given the importance of that role, John's humility must be one of the most important features of his character.

In comparing the Baptizer and the Messiah, several contrasts become readily apparent:

John was only a voice (**John 1:23**). Jesus was the Word (**1:1**).

John was merely a lamp (**5:35**). Jesus was the Light (**1:5**).

John baptized with water for repentance (**1:26**). Jesus baptized in the Holy Spirit (**1:33**).

John was a man, sent from God (**1:6**). Jesus was God become Man, the Lamb of God who takes away the sin of the world (**1:29**).

As John testified on two separate occasions, he knew Jesus as the Lamb of God. Especially because he was the son of Zechariah the priest, John surely understood the imagery conveyed by those words. Many Old Testament prophets described the Messiah as a lamb—meek, gentle, loving, and innocent. The blood of the lamb saved God's Old Testament people from the angel of death as they prepared for their release from the Egyptian bondage. The sacrificial system of the temple reinforced the truth that **"without the shedding of blood there is no forgiveness" (Heb. 9:22).**

During the intertestamental period, the people of Israel began to use the lamb in a new way—as a symbol of power. Oppressed by their enemies, the Jewish nation adopted the horned lamb as a representation of the conquering power of God, the Champion of God. This imagery is echoed by the apostle John in the Revelation (5:6-14; 6:1; 7:9; etc.)

As William Barclay states, "In one word (lamb), John sums up the love, the sacrifice, the suffering, and the triumph of Christ" (The Gospel of John, vol. 1, p. 82).

GETTING INTO THE LESSON

Talk about "mistaken identity" using the introductory material in the Student Book. Lead into the idea that today people still misunderstand Jesus and mistake His identity. Yet John carefully introduces His gospel in such a way as to emphasize Jesus' identify from the very beginning.

WE ARE ALL WITNESSES (Objective 1)

If the students have read the assigned text before class, you can ask them to skim it again to find the information called for in the Student Book. Let them do this independently and then compare answers.

Answers to the questions should be self-evident from the texts given. Question d calls for students' opinions. Stress the idea that despite our seeming sophistication, people today still try to escape responsibility for their own sin and failure. John would probably be no more popular today than he was at the time of Christ.

THE LAMB OF GOD (Objectives 2 and 3)

Spend more time on this part of the lesson. Develop the Old Testament concept of blood atonement, especially as it related to the Passover celebration. Many parallels can be drawn.

See the discussion of some of these found in the Concordia Self-Study Commentary, page 68.

WHO IS JESUS? (Objectives 2 and 3)

Have individual students find each reference and read the words aloud. The students should record their answers to the questions in their books.

Then talk about possible responses people make to this very important question today. One very popular idea you will want to help the students work through portrays Jesus as a great moral, ethical teacher—but not as God the Son.

Tell why this cannot be a valid opinion. Jesus claimed on numerous occasions to be divine as well as human. If Jesus was not really God, we have two options:

1. Jesus was a charlatan who claimed to be divine but knew in fact He was not. Thus He deliberately exploited the gullible crowds for His own ends. If this is true, Jesus certainly could not have been a great teacher of moral principles, but rather a great hypocrite.

2. Jesus actually believed Himself to be divine, but was in fact deluded. But if Jesus truly thought Himself to be God when He was in fact not, then we must conclude that He was insane. We must judge Him in the same

way we would judge someone who made that claim today as completely out of touch with reality.

So then, since a great moral teacher could be neither a liar and charlatan nor mentally deranged, no one can dismiss Jesus as merely a great moral teacher. Our Lord did not leave this option open to us. He didn't intend to. Either He was and is God as He claimed, or He was a liar or worse. Christians, of course, believe Jesus to be true God and true Man.

Let the students share with one another the papers they began in session 6. As they do this, help individual students with content in the ways this guide suggested in session 6.

Reading assignment for next time: John 2:1-11

Session 9: Jesus' First Sign

BIBLE BASIS: John 2:1-11

CENTRAL TRUTH

Jesus acts in human history in His own time and in His own way. Yet in mercy and compassion, He always works for the good of His children. All history serves to bring glory and honor to God and vindication to His children.

OBJECTIVES

That the students will:
1. Describe Jesus' miracles as signs or evidences, pointing to His divinity
2. Patiently trust God's power and loving purpose to be revealed in their own lives
3. Tell how God is at work in both the ordinary and extraordinary events of their daily lives

BACKGROUND

John records only nine of Jesus' miraculous acts. The account of His changing of the water into wine at Cana appears only in John's gospel. The apostle uses this miracle to focus our attention on Christ's authority and His divine power. Again, from the beginning of the book, we see Jesus' true identity revealed in the gospel of John.

The key verse is 2:11. All the supernatural events the gospel writer chose to record demonstrate God's power. They serve as "sign posts" pointing out the truth about Jesus' identity, His authority, and His compassion.

Just as the Savior revealed Himself on this occasion, so He continues to reveal His power and glory throughout history. Yet, we dare never try to squeeze Him into our human ideas about how and when He should act on our behalf.

John's use of the term hour (first explained in session 4) should prove useful as you lead your students to an understanding of the truths of this narrative. God's timetable doesn't always coincide with our preconceived notions. Even Jesus' mother did not fully understand. Yet as we begin to grasp the truth of who Jesus really is, our faith grows firmer and relies more deeply upon Jesus' wisdom, power, and compassion to help us in our every need.

GETTING INTO THE LESSON

Introduce the lesson by inviting responses to the question, **Have you ever experienced a miracle?**

Work into a discussion as to the meaning of the word miracle. **What makes an event a miracle?** Have students consult dictionaries available in your classroom. After students have had adequate time to think through their own personal opinions, suggest a general working definition that miracles are "special events in which God's power and glory can be seen through the eyes of faith." Do they agree or disagree? Postpone discussion until later in the period.

Review the meaning of the word sign as you first encountered it in the sense John uses it (see session 4).

FOLLOWING THE SIGNS (Objective 1)

Let the students read the account from **John 2:1-11**. Assign class members to read the dialog as though they were the various characters in the narrative. You will also need a narrator to read any material that is not dialog.

Then allow a few minutes for the students to jot questions and comments in their notebooks. Talk about these as time and student interest permit. Be sure everyone understands the basic factual events of the narrative. If some students would benefit from a discussion of wedding customs at the time of Christ, share some of this information with them.

IT'S ABOUT TIME . . . (Objectives 2 and 3)

Briefly discuss the various meanings for time implied in the sentences from the Student Book. Also have the students review the comments in session 4 referring to Jesus' hour.

Remind the class once again that throughout his gospel, John stresses Jesus' concern for His hour, His time. In doing so, John emphasizes the Savior's commitment to doing His Father's will. Not only does Jesus obey the heavenly Father, but He does so according to a divine timetable. His entire life follows a planned sequence of divinely ordered appointments.

The last paragraph in this section in the Student Book deals with the fact that we often prescribe to God how and when He should respond to our needs and to our prayers. Our preferences may not always coincide with the Father's will for us. When we wait for Him to act on our behalf, we can trust Him to work in all things for our good.

Be sure that as you talk about God's will, the students understand that God's Word reveals His will for many areas of our lives--"big" or "little." We don't need to guess His will when He has revealed it. At other times, His Word has not spoken directly to our specific problem. At those times, we pray for His will to be done, knowing that His will is "good and perfect."

DOES GOD KNOW? DOES HE CARE?
(Objectives 2 and 3)

Read through the vignette in class. Discuss Judy's problems together. You may want to list on the chalkboard the various difficult circumstances she faces. Does Judy need a miracle? How could (might) God intervene to help her? How might He use you, a classmate, to help Judy?

Then talk about circumstances and how they sometimes affect us. Several applications may be drawn:

a. If we depend on circumstances for our joy rather than on Jesus, we will never find true peace and happiness.

b. Our God is so very kind and loving that He is both willing **and** able to bring great good out of even the most terrible circumstances.

c. God uses seemingly adverse situations in our lives to help us grow more mature, more patient, and more confident in His love and care.

Try to get the students to suggest some possible positive solutions to Judy's problem.

The more difficult next step, of course, involves having the class jot down negative circumstances they face in their own individual lives right now. How are these negative situations affecting them? If worry and fear are sins, what can we as God's people do to conquer them? Stress God's willingness both to forgive our sins and to cleanse us from all unrighteousness. We can use His power to overcome the sin in our lives. This all happens by God's grace, not as a result of our trying harder. In what way is this a miracle? Talk about it in light of the definition you developed earlier in the class period.

Finally ask, **How might the Bible verse printed at the top of this lesson help us use God's power?**

Reading assignment for next time: **John 2:12-24**

Session 10: Jesus--the Temple of God

BIBLE BASIS: John 2:12-24

CENTRAL TRUTH

Jesus spoke and acted with authority that came directly from God His Father. The Father's glory indwelled Him. In grace, God desires to make us temples for His righteousness and glory as He enables us to submit to His authority.

OBJECTIVES

That the students will:

1. Better understand Jesus' motives and authority as He cleansed the temple

2. Hear Jesus' call to be temples of the living God and repent for times they have desecrated this temple by sinning

3. Respect Jesus' authority and submit to it in willing obedience as the Holy Spirit empowers them

BACKGROUND

"You can't make me!" Perhaps at some times in your teaching career you have encountered a student who challenged your authority in just such a pointed way. Perhaps, too, you have had students who by quiet noncompliance challenged your role less obviously but just as certainly. Either way, the challenge demanded that you assert your authority and reassume a position of leadership.

"Who gave you the right to do this?" The Scribes and Pharisees, infuriated by Jesus' actions in driving the money changers from the temple, angrily challenged the Savior. Just as these same leaders had questioned John the Baptizer's authority **(John 1:19—28),** so now they demanded a miraculous sign from the Savior.

Instead of a sign, Jesus gave them a promise--**"Destroy this temple,"** He prophesied, **"and I will raise it again in three days."** His response pointed to the final sign He would give to the Jewish nation and to the whole world. It would be the sign to end all signs. Each miracle John records in His gospel lies along the path to Jesus' empty tomb.

For those who cared to hear, the Lord's promise warned of coming judgment and urged sinners to repentance. The temple, glorious as it was, would be destroyed. The shadows and types of the Old Testament sacrificial system would be abolished when the Lamb of God was slaughtered as the final, once-for-all sacrifice for sin.

When that happened, the building that had housed the symbols of the Old Covenant would no longer be needed. No earthly building could hold the spectacular love of God. The play on words Jesus used implied much more than a commentary on the temple building itself. God Himself has lived among us **(John 1:14).** He is Immanuel who now reigns at the right hand of the Father **(Heb. 1:3).** This same Lord who became our Savior now desires to live in us! He desires to make us temples of the living God!

The Lord asserts His authority in our lives, not from a desire to dominate, but rather from a yearning love that seeks to glorify His creatures by making us the objects of that love.

Nevertheless, His claims to authority challenge adolescents who naturally seek independence from all authority and external control. As they struggle with establishing their own identity, the claims of Christ can seem a threat.

We need to help them discover that the rule of God does not involve coercion or manipulation. Nor does it involve a temporary commitment God wheedles from His creatures by performing "quick fix" miracles designed to seduce us against our will.

Rather, God's Spirit moves to draw us to our Father by His love, to dwell within us, and to empower us to manifest His glory to those around us. As we become more mature in Christ we will reflect this glory more and more as temples where His Spirit dwells.

GETTING INTO THE LESSON (Objective 1)

To help students understand the furor Jesus caused by His actions in today's Bible narrative, give them some background information about the temple itself and the sacrificial system carried on there. A good Bible dictionary will prove helpful. As an alternative, you could assign research about Herod's temple to one or more students as homework prior to today's class. Share the report with the group.

You will also want to clarify for the class the timing of this incident. The synoptic writers place Jesus' cleansing of the temple after Palm Sunday and before His passion. John places it at the beginning of His ministry. Some Bible scholars have argued that John rearranged the chronology to better suit His theological purposes. A simpler explanation is that the Lord cleansed the temple twice—once at the beginning and once at the end of His ministry. Nothing in the text would militate against such an explanation and it avoids the many "mental gymnastics" required if we assume that John altered facts to fit his presuppositions. While you will not want to spend much time on this in class, be sure that students are aware of the differences between John's record and the incident reported by the writers of the synoptic gospels.

BY WHOSE AUTHORITY? (Objective 1)

Today's narrative communicates the Scriptural Law/Gospel message with crystal clarity. As you discuss Jesus' authority, talk with the class about what makes it so difficult for us to submit willingly to the authority over us--even to God's. We were by nature rebellious. Even now, as God's new creatures, our flesh rebels at times against our Father's right to direct our lives.

As you discuss God's character, help the students understand that God is both a God of justice and a God of mercy. Mercy continues to reach out to us even when we walk away in rebellion. Yet, a day of justice will come someday for those who refuse mercy. God must (and does) punish sin. We misrepresent God if we fail to teach either one of these two aspects of His character.

THE TEMPLE OF THE LORD (Objectives 2 and 3)

Each paragraph in this section includes information and a question or two designed to promote class discussion.

1. Students without much background in Old Testament history will need help as they interpret Jeremiah's message. Remind the class that the temple to which the prophet refers was one of a series of buildings in which Israel worshiped at various times in history. Built originally to glorify God, the temple became the object of Israel's confidence. After all, how could a foreign nation harm them as long as the temple stood in Jerusalem? God found this attitude totally repugnant.

2. At the time of Christ, Israel's attitude and devotional life had not improved. Once again, the rebuilt temple and the sacrificial system it represented had become objects of veneration--idols.

While beautiful buildings, liturgical forms, and other aids can add greatly to our times of praise and worship, we need to take care to focus on God, not on the worship aids themselves. Students may think of other applications.

3. Refer students to **1 Cor. 15:17** and/or **Rom. 4:25**. Stress the truth that Jesus' resurrection sealed God's pardon for our sins and His promise that because Jesus lives, so will we.

4. In the New Testament church, God's people are His temples. Explore with the class various implications of that fact. **Rom. 8** mentions nearly a dozen benefits we receive from this relationship with God. Other New Testament references add still more benefits. As you close today, ask the students to say a silent prayer of thanksgiving for some of these benefits.

Assignment for next time: Test on sessions 1--10. Students should reread **John 1** and **2**.

Session 11: Concluding Activities for Unit 1

BIBLE BASIS: John 1--2

The material that follows suggests possible ways to evaluate students' progress and understanding. You may or may not wish to administer a written test to your class. If you find a better way to evaluate the progress of your class, by all means use it. Not all teaching situations call for a written evaluation. The material here is optional and may be adapted for use at another time--later in the course or with another class at a later date. Your instructional circumstances should determine when and how you can both teach and evaluate most effectively.

In the same way, your teaching style and Scriptural emphases may vary from that of other teachers in other classrooms and from year to year within the same school. Therefore if you decide to give a written test, it will be unique to a certain extent. Use the questions suggested below as a resource when you write your own test. Be sure to include questions aimed at evaluating student knowledge, understanding, and practical application of Biblical truth to daily life.

You may want to allow students to use their notebooks as they take the test. This will encourage students to complete their homework and to take good notes. In any case, you should check the individual notebooks as a part of your total evaluation of student work during this unit.

SUGGESTED MULTIPLE CHOICE QUESTIONS

1. John, the gospel writer, was also the writer of (a) Acts (b) Romans (c) 1 Corinthians (d) Revelation **(d)**

2. The symbol often used for John's gospel is (a) an eagle (b) an eye (c) a bull (d) a lamb **(a)**

3. The author John was (a) born in Nazareth (b) the brother of James, a son of Zebedee (c) not one of Jesus' 12 original disciples (d) the man who baptized Jesus **(b)**

4. The first gospel to be written was probably (a) Matthew (b) Mark (c) Luke (d) John **(b)**

5. John wrote his gospel around (a) AD 40 (b) AD 55 (c) AD 90 (d) AD 125 **(c)**

6. The word gospel means (a) love (b) God (c) light (d) good news **(d)**

7. Miracles are called signs in John because (a) they help us see and recognize Jesus (b) they warn us of eternal damnation (c) they light the path to heaven (d) they all pointed to John the Baptizer **(a)**

8. John stresses Jesus' relationship to God the Father. Therefore we could best refer to his gospel account as being (a) synoptic (b) progressive (c) historical (d) theological **(d)**

9. John tells us that he wrote to (a) proclaim that Jesus is the Messiah, the Son of God (b) tell of the history of Jesus (c) record the history of the Church (d) disprove inaccurate theories of Jesus **(a)**

10. Matthew, Mark, and Luke are called synoptic gospels because they (a) clearly tell about Jesus (b) are similar in their outline and content about Jesus (c) were written by Gentile Christians (d) contain no parables **(b)**

11. John points to Jesus' real "Hour of Glory" as His (a) baptism (b) ascension (c) death (d) first miracle **(c)**

12. John does not record (a) Jesus' ascension (b) Christ before Pontius Pilate (c) any miracles (d) Jesus' first miracle **(a)**

13. For John, to believe in Jesus means to (a) understand Him to be God's Son and trust Him for salvation (b) doubt His power but listen to Him (c) acknowledge that God exists (d) know for a fact Jesus was a human being **(a)**

14. John's gospel begins with (a) Jesus' birth in Bethlehem (b) the family of Joseph and Mary (c) a miracle by John the Baptizer (d) a statement about Jesus being the Word of God **(d)**

15. The first miraculous sign performed by Jesus was (a) raising Lazarus from the dead (b) raising

Himself from the dead (c) walking on the water (d) changing water into wine **(d)**

16. <u>Synoptic</u> means (a) to share your faith (b) to see together or alike (c) good news for all (d) to tell the truth **(b)**

17. The phrase "Word of God" can refer to (a) Jesus (b) miracles (c) signs (d) believing in Jesus **(a)**

18. The "wrath of God" refers to (a) the power to do miracles (b) Jesus Christ, God's Son (c) God's anger over man's sin (d) God's proclamation of forgiveness **(c)**

19. A proper parallel for Law and Gospel is (a) judgment and grace (b) Old Testament and New Testament (c) Jews and Gentiles (d) obedience and disobedience **(a)**

SUGGESTED SHORT ANSWER QUESTIONS

Write your answers using complete sentences. Explain your ideas clearly.

1. John calls Jesus the <u>Logos</u>. How was Jesus a <u>Logos?</u> Why does John call Him that?

2. Choose one of the paragraphs below. Read it. Then write your reaction to the statement. Be as complete as possible in your answer.

  a. "<u>Jesus should perform dramatic miracles in our lives today. Then people would not doubt and disbelieve. The miracles would demonstrate God's power and prove to the people that He actually is the Son of God and Messiah!</u>"

  b. "<u>Jesus was a very good man. He taught people God's Word. He did kind, good things for everyone. He is our greatest example for how to live as God's children.</u>"

3. Think about the term "<u>The law of God.</u>"

  a. What is it? To what does this term refer?

  b. What is the purpose of God's law in our lives?

  c. From your experience of God's law, tell how God's law makes you feel and react.

  d. How is the "Gospel of Jesus Christ" the solution to our problems as we face God's law?

4. Why does John call miracles <u>signs</u>?

5. Identify three experiences from your recent past that have reminded you that you are a sinner and are imperfect. Each one should be unique and different from the others.

6. Why is John's gospel not called one of the synoptics? Describe in general terms how it differs from the other three gospel accounts.

7. Why is the <u>hour</u> of Jesus' death an hour of <u>glory</u> according to Jesus?

8. Jesus is called the <u>Lamb of God.</u> Explain why. Why is it important to you personally that He was the Lamb of God?

9. Imagine that you were a Jewish person who lived at the time of John the Baptizer and Jesus. You have heard John preach and have seen and heard some of what Jesus has done and said. Explain what your feelings and impressions might be of these two special people. Would you have believed in Jesus, the one who does miracles and wonders as the Messiah?

Feel free to duplicate the questions above for use in testing. Please add the following credit line: Concordia Publishing House. Copyright 1986.

Reading assignment for next time: **John 3:1-21** and **Numbers 21:4-9**

Unit 2: Jesus--the Way, the Truth, the Life

This unit includes a study of the bulk of Jesus' discourses from John's gospel. Some of the most beautiful statements the Savior spoke will be examined over the next several sessions.

Continue to personalize Jesus' message for your students as much as possible.

PLANNING THE UNIT

Session 14: Bring newspaper, magazine, or video ads to class. These should be beverage ads. See the lesson for further details.

Session 15: Plan a specific outreach assignment for your students to complete on their own.

Session 23: Two reference books about shepherds and their sheep are listed in the "**Background**" section of this lesson. You may want to get these or other similar references ahead of time.

Session 12: Born Again!

BIBLE BASIS: John 3:1-21

CENTRAL TRUTH

We cannot come to God on the basis of our own merit. We must be born again through the Holy Spirit's power. Those who by faith have been born again receive God's power and become His children through their personal relationship with Jesus Christ.

OBJECTIVES

That the students will:
1. Provide the Biblical meaning of the phrase "born again" and contrast this meaning with some contemporary secular understandings of the term
2. Describe the Spirit's role in giving the gift of faith in Jesus Christ
3. Use the power of the new life they have received from God to live lives of daily repentance and faith, bringing honor to Him

BACKGROUND

Most Christians probably feel somewhat familiar with the encounter between Jesus and Nicodemus. The account contains a variety of ideas, many of which involve contrasts:

<u>Law vs. Grace</u>
<u>Flesh vs. Spirit</u>
<u>Human wisdom vs. God's plan</u>
<u>Light vs. Darkness</u>
<u>Obedience vs. Rebirth</u>

These important accents combine to form a strong message about the true and only way any person may be saved. Sessions 12 and 13 will both deal with the account from **John 3**. As you plan for today's class session, you may wish to look ahead to the teaching suggestions for session 13 as well. Select those activities from both lessons which will best meet the needs of your students.

Nicodemus, caught up as he was in the pharisaical system of his time, understood his relationship with God in terms of obedience. From that point of view, God's expectations had been clearly defined. The **Torah** (the written law) and the **Talmud** (the oral tradition explicating the Torah) spelled out God's demands in detail. **"Do this and you shall live,"** Jesus Himself had said at one time to an expert in the Law (**Luke 10:28**).

Perhaps Nicodemus, like Luther, experienced lingering wisps of doubt. Perhaps guilt gnawed at his conscience. Perhaps he wondered if by some fluke, he may have overlooked a law or two. Nicodemus knew he was good. But how could he be sure he had been good enough?

Whatever drove Nicodemus to seek Jesus out, we can be sure the Rabbi's teaching about righteousness before God puzzled and frustrated him. The call to rebirth, to begin afresh, to be born of God--what kind of teaching was that? How could a mortal person hope to do that?

The Good News Jesus shared with Nicodemus was, of course, that mortal people--sinful people--could not. Life, eternal life, results as a gift of God's grace. Sinners needed regeneration and redemption, not merely reformation. Just as God's Old Testament people had been healed and restored physically as they looked in faith at Moses' bronze serpent, so all sinners receive new life and power to live as God's children as they come to Christ by faith.

The change that God initiates within us involves much more than a superficial reorganization of our priorities or habits. It is as basic as new life itself! The old is gone and the new has come, as Paul later wrote to the Corinthians.

As teens search for identity and purpose, God's love offers comfort and confident hope. Earthly measures of success, acceptance by peers, pressures of school work, and the frustrations of growing up in contemporary society, can be transformed in light of the new life your students have received. No problem and no joy stands outside the quality of life promised by the Gospel.

GETTING INTO THE LESSON (Objective 1)

The statements quoted in the Student Book convey some common misconceptions about the term "born again." Non-Christians have adopted the phrase and secularized it. Cults have adopted it in some cases. Even some Christians use the words wrongly--to make distinctions between levels of sanctification.

Have someone read each quotation. Allow some time for student comments. Ask if they have ever heard people outside the church use the phrase. Note that the second quotation was made by someone caught up in TM and caution your students against it.

RULES, RULES, AND MORE RULES (Objective 2)

Make the list describing the beliefs and characteristics of the Pharisees on the chalkboard or on a piece of poster paper. If time will not permit the additional research to be done in class, ask students to do this on their own. Or lecture briefly to explain points you feel important. Be sure students understand the legalism at the heart of their religion.

Any good Bible dictionary should adequately explain Torah and Talmud. Be sure students write the definitions in their own words--words they understand.

As you talk about the misconceptions betrayed in the quotations in the final part of this section, stress the truth that:

Christ + Anything = Nothing

If we add any human work to God's grace, it stops being grace. We are not saved because we go to church. We are not forgiven because we feel sorry enough. We are not acceptable to God because we have "cleaned up our act" before we come to Him. We do not earn God's love by what we do for His kingdom.

Discuss the statements compassionately, sharing with your students the despair and hopelessness that can develop when we fall into these errors. Some of your own students may believe they must feel sorry enough before God will forgive certain of their sins. Some of your students may suspect that, until they overcome specific vices, they cannot really be sure that God loves them. Others may feel themselves better than most teens because they attend a Christian school or because they teach Sunday school. Pray for the Spirit's help in applying Law and Gospel accurately.

A WHOLE NEW ME! (Objectives 2 and 3)

The discussion about being reborn resumes with a comparison to human infancy. Walk through it quickly with your students. The application once again is one of grace.

If your students did not read **Num. 21:4-9** before class, take time to do it now. Israel did not deserve the healing God provided. We do not deserve the redemption Jesus won. We are saved not because we are good, but because He is!

BORN AGAIN! (Objective 3)

1. Return once more to the statements at the beginning of the lesson. Use the questions in the Student Book to discuss them. Go beyond helping students point out factual errors in the statements. Theology can never be separated from real-life application. Ask the class what difference this misunderstanding of God's truth makes. (Refer back to **John 3:5** if necessary.)

2. Assign the paragraph as homework. Be sure to read the students' responses soon after they write them. As you read, you may discover some opportunities for personal ministry to individuals. Be alert to this possibility.

3. Students with artistic ability may want to design a poster or bulletin board using the slogan here.

Reading assignment for next time:

John 3:1-21

Suggest that as students reread the text assigned for today, they read it in light of today's class discussion. Ask them to jot down any remaining questions they have about Jesus' words.

Session 13: The Light of His Love

BIBLE BASIS: John 3:1-21

CENTRAL TRUTH

Jesus is the Light of the world. This Light exposes the darkness of sin in human lives. It also comforts the believer who lives confidently in the light of God's love and forgiveness.

OBJECTIVES

That the students will:
1. Describe the symbolic relationship in Scripture between darkness/sin and light/truth
2. Identify that God's ultimate purpose in Jesus is to save sinners, not to condemn them
3. Experience God's acceptance of them in Jesus Christ as unconditional and eternal
4. Use confession/absolution more meaningfully to defeat sin in their lives

BACKGROUND

The story is told of a young man who visited a famous art gallery. A few hours later, after gazing at priceless treasures from many centuries and after viewing some of the world's finest masterpieces, the man was approached by the curator who asked for his comments.

The young man responded, "I guess I don't think much of all your old pictures."

The curator shrugged and quietly noted, "The art here is no longer on trial. But those who view it are."

This story, first told by William Barclay, illustrates the truth about sinners who confront Jesus Christ. Many stand before the Lord of heaven and earth and fail to see any light, love, or power. In rebellious ignorance, sinners thus judge themselves. As Jesus said, **"Whoever does not believe is condemned already."** The Light is not on trial—but rather the sinner who loves darkness.

As the young people in your class search for their true identity, they need not fear the light that Jesus brings. Because of what the Savior has done for us, because He accepts and loves us unconditionally, we can face with honesty the rebellion against God that still clings to us. We can admit our sin. Because God has made us new creatures by His marvelous grace, we need not hide our failures and our weaknesses from Him or from one another. We need not conceal the dark places in our hearts.

Instead, we can invite the One who is the Light to expose and scatter the darkness. The dynamic power found in confession and God's absolution is released to do its sanctifying work in our hearts. We receive joy and peace. He received honor and glory. How good God is!

GETTING INTO THE LESSON (Objective 1)

Read through the introductory material in the Student Book. Have students name movies or books they have seen or read recently that revolve around the concept of dualism. Mention that the Christian faith rejects this philosophy because we know our God will be victorious. Satan truly is powerful, but God is almighty! There's quite a difference.

IT'S DARK IN HERE! (Objectives 2, 3, and 4)

Give students a few minutes to complete each of the two exercises in this section. Ask volunteers to share, not necessarily the episode itself, but the feelings they jotted down.

Assign the passages from John's gospel to individual groups of students. Have the verses read one immediately after the other. Be sure each student knows what to read when. Select good readers to do this. You should attempt to have the words build to a kind of crescendo. If possible, repeat the reading a second time. After the readers have had a chance to practice once, the reading should be even more dramatic.

Share the story from the "Background" section of this guide and comment on its meaning. Then discuss why human beings so often love the darkness.

The light Jesus brings:

1. Exposes our sin; it reveals the ugly things we think, say, and do.

2. Scatters the darkness as He forgives and helps us deal with the sin the light has exposed.

This would be an excellent time to talk about repentance, confession, and forgiveness. Consider making the following points with your class.

a. By themselves, even Christians can't repent for sin. Repentance is a gift from God (**Acts 5:31; 2 Cor. 7:8-10;** etc.).

b. When the Holy Spirit convicts us of sin, we confess it to God. Confession is not feeling bad about ourselves for three days until we've felt bad enough, long enough. Confession is not making God feel sorry for us because we feel so miserably guilty. Confession is not a negative, terrible thing that hurts us. Rather, it involves saying what God says about our sin--that we have done wrong, that it hurts us and our relationship with Him, and that we don't want it in our lives anymore. (The Greek word for confess means "to speak together"--we agree with God when we confess.)

c. Sometimes, when we confess sin to God, we also need to confess to the person whom our sin has hurt. That's not an easy thing to do. God does not ask us to do this to hurt us, but because it helps us and it keeps bitterness and anger from building up and festering in us and in other people.

d. When we confess our sins, God always, always forgives us. It doesn't matter how often we have done that particular thing. It doesn't matter how terrible we think the sin is. God's grace is always bigger than all our sin.

Also, in forgiving us, God forgets the offense. He will never bring it up to us again. Satan might. Our own conscience might. Other people might. But God never will, because when He forgives a sin--it's gone forever. By the Holy Spirit's power, we can forgive ourselves just as God has forgiven us.

e. Even though sometimes we might think of confessing sin as a negative experience, actually it's a victorious one. When we ask God's forgiveness, He also gives us His power to overcome the sins that are hurting us. Confession is a powerful tool the Holy Spirit has given us to defeat the sin in our lives and to become more and more like Jesus.

f. <u>Grace</u> is the key word. By God's grace, we are led to contrition and repentance. By God's grace we are enabled to confess our sins to God and to one another. By God's grace we are forgiven and our sin is blotted out. By God's grace, we receive power to live as the new creatures He has made us.

CONFUSION AND CONFESSION (Objectives 3 and 4)

Discuss the brief story about Judy in the Student Book. The class may recognize her from session 9.

Like Judy, most people (and sadly, even many Christians) are fearful of others discovering what they are really like.

Ask the class how Judy was "in the light," yet also "in the darkness." Encourage the class to apply to Judy's life the concepts of repentance and confession they reviewed earlier in the session. How might these ideas "turn on the light" for her? How might they do the same for your students?

OPTIONAL ACTIVITIES

As extra credit or as part of a regular assignment for the whole class, you could assign one of the activities below.

1. Light is a major theme in John's gospel. Have students design a poster based on the phrase "In the Light of His Love." The sketch in the

Student Book is one example of how this might be done. Tell students that color, creativity, originality, and neatness are all important.

2. Have each student write a one-page letter to Judy. What comfort could they offer? Perhaps students know an actual person facing a similar problem right now. Invite them to write to that special person instead. Encourage them to be sure the Gospel is clear and personal.

Reading assignment for next time: John 4:1-26

Session 14: Quenching Your Thirst

BIBLE BASIS: John 4:1-26

CENTRAL TRUTH

A personal relationship with Jesus Christ offers the believer a peace and joy that may not be found in any human relationship, experience, or achievement. Jesus is truly the Living Water that satisfies our thirst.

OBJECTIVES

That the students will:
1. Explain the Samaritan/Jewish conflict that forms the backdrop for this incident
2. Describe how the love of God in Jesus Christ fulfills people's deepest need in the only true and lasting way
3. Define "living water"
4. Become springs of living water for those around them in school and in their families

BACKGROUND

As he studied human potential and human happiness, the psychologist Abraham Maslow identified five basic levels of need he believes all human beings share. Maslow believes each of these five levels builds on the one below in a kind of "needs pyramid." Until the needs on all five levels have been met, we cannot be the full, complete human beings we have the potential to be. In ascending order, Maslow has defined these levels as: physical needs; safety needs; the need for social acceptance; the need for self-esteem; and the need for self-actualization (fulfillment).

Maslow's hierarchy provides an interesting context for the proclamation of the Gospel. While the theory does not contradict a Christian understanding of human beings, it lacks an emphasis on the spiritual nature of our needs. All human beings do, indeed, have deep spiritual needs and each individual in our world, knowingly or unknowingly, seeks ways to meet those spiritual needs. Some ways are positive. Some are negative.

The Samaritan woman Jesus met at the well had deep-seated spiritual needs. She may or may not have been aware of them. Yet, when Jesus began to speak with her--to confront her with God's Law, her sin, and with His grace--she apparently recognized the gnawing hole of loneliness and guilt in the center of her existence. She recognized a thirst for the living water only He could give.

It may be that some (or many) of your students have begun to question the meaning of their lives. <u>Where am I going? What will make me happy? What makes life satisfying?</u> Society screams all kinds of answers in response to these questions. Yet, as Jesus told the woman at the well, only the living water He gives will quench human thirst--quench it fully and eternally. His pardon, His peace, His power come to us freely by His grace. He is the Source of the new life, the eternal life that springs up within us as the Holy Spirit works in our hearts.

Even beyond quenching our own thirst, God wants to transform our lives into springs of refreshment to others who thirst. We can share the living water because we know its Source--Jesus Christ. What meaning and purpose that gives to our lives! What significance our lives can have!

Before you teach today, pray that the Holy Spirit would use you to refresh some dry places in your students' hearts as you share the Living Water with them.

GETTING INTO THE LESSON (Objective 2)

If possible, bring beverage ads like those described in the Student Book, to class. Use videotape, cassette tape, and/or an opaque projector to share the ads you find. Or simply allow students to think of slogans on their own. The last two paragraphs in the section hint at the main point of the lesson. Help the class understand the directions and mark their lists. Avoid further comment until later.

JESUS, THE LIVING WATER (Objectives 1 and 3)

1. Use the sentence completion exercise to clarify the facts of the Bible narrative. The statements bring out several peripheral truths as well:

--Jesus was true man, as well as true God. He became tired and thirsty like other human beings.

--The woman felt surprised at the Lord's request because He, a male and a rabbi, would speak to her. She also felt surprised because He, a Jew, would have anything to do with her, a Samaritan.

--The hatred between Jews and Samaritans began already back at the time of Ezra and Nehemiah. See a good Bible dictionary for additional background facts to share with students.

--Jesus knew about her five husbands and about her life of adultery at present. Gently, but in a way she could not ignore, He confronted her with her sin.

--Worship, Jesus said, must be "worship in spirit and in truth." Worship spills out of a heart full of love and adoration for God.

--Jesus promised the woman living water. The students should struggle a bit with what He meant. What need was Jesus offering to fill for her? This is the Gospel presentation that accompanied the Law He also spoke.

2. These questions have been designed to help the students define the woman's needs and the ways in which she was trying to fill them. Had she found true joy and peace? How do we know?

I'M THIRSTY (Objective 2)

Jacob's well in Samaria may seem very removed in time and place from the lives of your students. The point of this section is to help your students identify the needs that people face today. You will want to help your class to discover that basic human needs don't change much throughout history. The language we use to describe our needs might, but the needs themselves do not.

1. Share Maslow's list with the class after they have developed their class list. Place both on chart paper or on the chalkboard where all students can see them.

2. Discuss the lists using the questions printed in the Student Book.

3. At this time you will want to go back to the beverage slogans the class identified at the beginning of the class period. Soft drink ads sometimes promise more than they can deliver. **Do other advertisements do this too? Why might this be? Why can't _things_ make people happy?** Encourage students to think of their lists of needs while they answer this.

WHAT WILL SATISFY ME? (Objectives 2, 3, and 4)

1. Finally, the lesson personalizes the truths of the text. Each student is asked to draw up a list of personal needs. Help them think of ways other people have tried to quench these same thirsts and ask students to comment on the degree to which the "thirst quenchers" that people suggest really work. Do they lead to happiness, joy, peace, etc.?

From what they know about current events, what evidence is there that people are searching for, yet not finding, happiness? What could cause someone searching for happiness to commit suicide? Why is this not a satisfying answer to unhappiness?

2. The texts listed expand on Jesus' meaning for the term <u>Living Water</u>.

3. Be sure students answer as specifically as possible when discussing ways they can become springs of living water for others.

<u>Reading assignment for next time:</u>   John 4:1-42

Session 15: Sharing the Living Water

BIBLE BASIS: John 4:1-42

CENTRAL TRUTH

A personal relationship with Jesus Christ offers the believer a peace and joy that may not be found in any human relationship, experience, or achievement. Jesus truly is the Living Water that satisfies our thirst. Empowered by His Holy Spirit, we share that Living Water with others.

OBJECTIVES

That the students will:
1. Identify people around them who need the Living Water only Jesus can provide
2. Confront their own sinful reluctance to share the Good News of salvation with others and repent
3. List specific strategies they can use to share the Gospel with those who do not already know Jesus as Savior and Friend

BACKGROUND

This lesson extends the discussion of John 4:1-42 you began last time. As the Samaritan woman discovered, the quenching power of the Gospel is real and it works! Other "waters" satisfy various human needs temporarily. But our deepest needs, our spiritual needs, can only be satisfied as through Jesus Christ we come into a right relationship with our Creator and become a part of the heavenly Father's family.

Once we make that discovery, we can't help but share it. We can imagine the Samaritan woman, perhaps almost running, returning to the village to find her neighbors, friends, and even total strangers. "Can it be?" she asks. "Can this Man be the Messiah? He told me everything! Everything I've ever done! I believe He's the One—the One sent from God."

Who could keep such a discovery to themselves?

As the Savior looked up to see the crowds coming with the woman-turned-missionary, His heart must have melted with joy and urgency. After all, this is why He had come! The fields were white for harvest! The reaping had begun!

And it continues. Jesus calls you and your students to work in His fields to gather in the harvest. Today's lesson has been designed to help you equip your students to do that effectively. This guide suggests a number of ways to encourage, diffuse fears, and instruct students in ways to witness to their faith in Jesus. Read through them and select the procedures that will be of most help to your particular group at this stage in their spiritual growth.

THINKING ABOUT SHARING (Objective 2)

Use the discussion questions and the hypothetical story given in the Student Book to draw students into a discussion of witnessing in general. You want to stress the idea that finding water in a desperate situation like the one described would be very good news indeed. We would certainly want to share it. And we would feel very disappointed if the people whom we told rejected our good news in anger or by ridiculing us.

WE HAVE GOOD NEWS! (Objective 2)

Fear of being thought of as a "fanatic," fear of rejection, fear of failure, laziness, disinterest in the eternal welfare of others—all these sins lead us to ignore our responsibility to be about our Father's business in the harvest fields.

Lead students to recognize these factors as sin in their own lives. Point them once again to the power in confession, repentance, and the forgiveness Christ freely offers us—even for sins like these. His Spirit must enable us to both want to witness and to actually do the work of witnessing.

The second reason for not telling others about God's Good News involves a lack of knowledge of how to do it. Talk about any "equipping experiences" your students may have had. If some have gone along with their congregation's evangelism teams to visit homes or if some have taken surveys in connection with a program of youth evangelism, let these students share some of their experiences.

A CASE STUDY (Objective 3)

One way we learn how to share with others is by watching or listening to how it's done. **John 4** records a confrontation Jesus had with the woman of Sychar. Have the students read the account again, this time with an eye toward how Jesus organized His presentation of the Good News. Have them note especially how He used Law and Gospel in His talk with her.

Points you may want to note if your students do not, include the following:

Jesus chose a place He and the woman could talk quietly with little chance of interruption.

He drew her into friendly conversation about something she felt interested in.

He reminded her in a gentle, but firm way that she was a sinner.

He clearly proclaimed to her the Good News that He was the Savior, the Messiah.

WHO NEEDS GOOD NEWS? (Objectives 1 and 3)

Use this section to explain briefly the difference between the casual kinds of witnessing that go on in our daily conversation as we have opportunity and the more formal kinds of presentations we give as we explain the whole plan of salvation to someone who does not know it.

Have students think of someone with whom they might use the presentation they develop. Whether they actually do or not depends on the maturity of your group and their previous experiences, as well as the time you have available to devote to this kind of project.

A number of options are available:
1. Let students develop a Gospel presentation based on the ideas and Scripture verses given in the Student Book. Roleplay these presentations during the class session. Be sure everyone gets a chance to give an oral presentation. Critique each together, but be sure to stress the positive aspects of each individual's work. It would be good if you were to put your own comments in writing so the students could read them again after class.

2. Have students plan a personal presentation in class, practice it, and then present it to someone in their family--presumably someone who is already a Christian, but perhaps not--at the student's discretion. Have them report back to you orally or in writing. Use the "reporting time" as an opportunity to encourage them and to pray for them.

3. Ask students to interview 2, 5, or 10 people to ask, "What makes someone a Christian?" or "What do you think it means to be born again?" Have them report their results to the class. They may be surprised by the kinds of responses they hear. Design a presentation together in class that could be used with someone who gives a typical response to the questions you have used. (<u>Consider asking students to record their interviews on tape for use in class. Have them assure the people being taped that they will remain anonymous.</u>) Shy students could interview younger children or family members.

If you assign one of these take-home projects, be sure to follow up on the results. Remind students that "success" does not depend on us. The Holy Spirit creates faith as we speak God's Word. We are called to be faithful witnesses and to leave the results to God's grace.

<u>Reading assignment for next time</u>: **John 6:1-15 and 25-69**

Session 16: I Am the Bread of Life (Part 1)

BIBLE BASIS: John 6:1-15 and 25-69

CENTRAL TRUTH

Jesus Christ is the Bread of life, who gives eternal life to the believer. God continues to nourish His people through His Word and as we participate in the body and blood of Jesus in the Eucharist.

OBJECTIVES

That the students will:

1. Tell what Jesus meant by calling Himself the Bread of life

2. Express some of the questions people sometimes have about Jesus as they hear the Gospel message and answer them

3. Participate more meaningfully in the Lord's Supper as they understand more fully the need for daily repentance and renewal of their faith

BACKGROUND

Quite frequently John records an event, miracle, or experience in his gospel and then uses the circumstance to introduce one of Jesus' discourses. That's what happens in chapter 6, as we first see Jesus feeding more than 5,000 people and then elaborating on His declaration, "I am the Bread of Life."

Jesus did not hesitate to challenge His disciples and the people in the crowds that followed Him to believe in Him as God's promised Messiah. While some believed and asked for nourishment from Him, others found His teachings too difficult. They chose to return to the lives they had known previously (John 6:66).

To believe the truth that Jesus is the Bread of life, our students must first understand the symbolic meaning in His statement. After they have understood the Savior's claim, they need the Holy Spirit's enabling power to trust and then live by this truth. Be sure to pray for both these things to happen during your class period today.

While this section of Scripture does not deal with the Lord's Supper directly, the words of Jesus foreshadow the institution of this Sacrament. As His claim "I am the Bread of life" indicates, our relationship with Him is an intimate and personal one. We "eat His flesh and drink His blood" as we live in union with Him. He lives in us and we in Him by faith. Later, when Christ institutes the Lord's Supper, this intimate relationship is clarified and its meaning strengthened still more as He shares His body and blood with His disciples and down through the centuries with all believers. We receive both forgiveness of sins and power to live lives filled with eternal joy, peace, power, love, purpose, and enthusiasm.

How can we translate these deep theological truths into meaningful, life-related principles for our students? As you pray and plan, consider this challenge. The Student Book suggests roleplaying a news conference to help introduce the story and Jesus' teachings in a novel way. As students share their own questions and insights, be ready to supplement their ideas with some of your own. Your main task, however, involves guiding the discussion so that the class senses some of the drama and excitement of Jesus' life and teaching.

You will want to read the materials for session 17 before you teach session 16. This will give you some idea of the content to stress today and the emphases you will want to make next time.

GETTING INTO THE LESSON (Objectives 1 and 2)

The introductory information given in the Student Book should help students recognize some of the confusion that must have been in the minds of Jesus' listeners as He taught the crowds and performed undeniable miracles. Work through the material in class quickly. Most students should be familiar with the antagonism between the Savior and the religious leaders of His day.

Explain that today they will participate in a "News Conference with Jesus of Nazareth." The experience will give them a chance to "interview" Jesus about what He did and said in the text they read for today. You may choose to play the part of Jesus yourself, or you may assign a student to play that role. (If you choose a student, that person will need to have a thorough understanding of the meaning of the text. Let the person know ahead of time, and help him/her prepare.)

Use the news conference to help students elaborate on their understanding of what took place and what Jesus meant by what He said to the crowds.

Prepare questions you consider crucial and be sure they are covered at some time during the news conference. Here are some suggestions:

Do You ever tire of the large crowds? Where do You find the strength to maintain Your schedule? Why do You call Yourself both Son of God and Son of man? How can You be both? Wasn't Your father Joseph, the carpenter? How can a carpenter's son be a prophet and miracle-worker? Is it true that many of Your followers have left You? How do You explain that? What do You mean by "eating Your flesh and drinking Your blood"? How can You call Yourself the "Bread of life"? Isn't that a bit confusing? What does it mean?

As you begin the conference, introduce "Jesus" to the class. Think about using a video recorder and camera together with a live microphone to add realism to the event. If possible, have "Jesus" wear a robe.

BREAD--THE STAFF OF LIFE (Objectives 1 and 3)

These questions and activities have been designed to help students understand background information essential to a thorough understanding of Jesus' teachings. Work through them with the class before your news conference.

MY RESPONSE (Objectives 1, 2, and 3)

The Student Book assigns a reaction paper to help students think through what happened at the news conference. This may be assigned as homework if time will not permit the paper to be completed in class. Be sure to collect and comment on the papers the students write. Or ask them to include their paper in their notebook.

Reading assignment for next time: John 6:1-15 and 25-69

Session 17:   I Am the Bread of Life (Part 2)

BIBLE BASIS: John 6:1-15 and 25-69

CENTRAL TRUTH

Jesus Christ is the Bread of life who gives eternal life to the believer. God continues to nourish His people through His Word and as we participate in the body and blood of Jesus in the Eucharist.

OBJECTIVES

That the students will:
1. Tell what Jesus meant when He called Himself the Bread of life
2. Explain the intimacy of their relationship with Jesus, using the Bread of life metaphor
3. Participate more meaningfully in the Lord's Supper as they understand more fully the need for repentance and daily renewal of their relationship with Jesus

BACKGROUND

In today's lesson we will reinforce and expand on the themes first presented in session 16. Today's lesson places more emphasis on the Lord's Supper as an extension of Jesus' meaning when He identified Himself as the Bread of life. The Savior's use of this metaphor foreshadows His later institution of the Sacrament. As the **"BACKGROUND"** section of session 16 explained, **John 6** does not teach directly about the Sacrament, but rather explains the intimate personal relationship that Jesus longs to have with each believer.

This intimacy is more fully explained later, as Christ says to His disciples, **"Take eat, this is My body . . . Take drink, this is My blood."** In the Sacrament, Jesus invites believers to share the benefits He won for us.

Still today the Lord continues to

invite us to truly celebrate His holy meal. Yet in many places, real joy seems absent from the Eucharist. Perhaps a lack of understanding about what really takes place at the Lord's Table fosters this joylessness. The young people you teach need a positive invitation to "take eat . . . take drink" of the real spiritual food Jesus offers us here.

The experience of communion with God and others in the body of Christ can provide your young people with a foundation for positive peer and family relationships. Teenagers confront many challenges--challenges at once both threatening and exciting. As they face these challenges, the Lord Jesus promises that whoever eats His flesh and drinks His blood remains in Him and He in them (6:56). His promise carries sufficient power to heal any depression, to soothe any family crisis, to empower us to face any personal challenge, and to restore any broken relationship. Jesus Himself is really present: "Sir," they said, 'From now on give us this bread'" (6:34).

GETTING INTO THE LESSON (Objective 1)

Use the introductory material given in the Student Book to begin your discussion about spiritual food. Note that if some students seem interested in the practice of fasting, you might refer them to appropriate reference books. The main focus of this part of the lesson, though, should rest on a review of Jesus statement, "I am the Bread of life."

You may also want to rehearse briefly God's revelation of Himself to Moses at the burning bush as the eternal I AM. Each time you discuss one of Jesus' I am statements in the sessions that follow, review this Old Testament connection. (See **Ex. 3:13-15**.)

REAL FOOD (Objectives 1 and 2)

The Student Book contains a series of questions that will help your class think through some of the more difficult teachings of Christ from **John 6**. You may wish to let the students use part of today's period for individual study on their own, while you move around the classrooom answering questions that individuals have about the assignment. Encourage students to write complete sentences and to give careful thought to their responses. Reserve some time at the end of the session for individuals to share specific questions or insights they gained. Or simply discuss the questions together in class.

If they write their answers, you will want to collect the students' notebooks to evaluate their answers and comment on the responses they have given.

For question 5, have the students underline the appropriate statements. If, however, students are using Bibles that remain in your classroom, you will want to caution them against such underlining.

TAKE EAT . . . TAKE DRINK
(Objectives 2 and 3)

This section of the lesson explains in some detail the relationship between **John 6:53-58** and Jesus' institution of the Lord's Supper later on in His ministry. If you discussed these verses in depth last time, this section will provide a review for your students. If time did not permit an adequate discussion or if some students found the concept of foreshadowing somewhat troublesome last time, use today's session to reinforce the concepts.

You may wish to have the students write their paragraph about a time the Lord's Supper was meaningful to them in their Student Books. On the other hand, it might be best to have them respond to this question in their notebooks. Whichever choice you make, be sure that you read and comment on each individual's response sometime soon. If some students volunteer to share their responses with the rest of the class, this should prove to be a valuable experience for the whole group. Set aside time for it.

KEY WORDS FOR THIS UNIT (Objectives 1 and 2)

This lesson lists the key words

for the unit. Deal with these as you have with the key words from other lessons. Have students consult Bible dictionaries to grasp more fully the Biblical meanings of these particular terms.

Reading assignment for next time: John 7:1-52

Session 18: A Growing Storm of Controversy

BIBLE BASIS: John 7:1-52

CENTRAL TRUTH

Jesus is the Christ, the Son of God whom the Father sent to be the Savior of the world. The Holy Spirit enables us to see Him as the Messiah and to overcome the things that would cause us to deny His lordship in our lives.

OBJECTIVES

That the students will:
1. Explain some of the reasons behind the growing antagonism the scribes and Pharisees showed toward Jesus
2. Identify things that keep them from seeing the truth about Christ in their own lives and repent of those things
3. Receive power from the Holy Spirit to live more and more completely under the lordship of Jesus

BACKGROUND

Is Jesus the Christ? This question tantalized many in Israel who longed for release from the tyranny of Roman rule. The question both threatened and frustrated others, particularly the scribes and Pharisees--the established religious leaders of the day. Looking back on Jesus' life, miracles, and teachings, we wonder at the marked unbelief of the religious establishment. Yet, Jesus Himself explained the reasons behind their stubbornness.

In the first place, the Lord's teachings challenged the very foundation of the system they had established. Jesus Himself had said that the work of God is simply to believe in the One whom He has sent. The Savior taught that no one keeps the Law. No one! How His comments must have stunned the Pharisees!

These people had made an entire career out of being good, out of being religious, out of trying to make themselves acceptable in God's sight.

Secondly, Jesus taught with authority. The crowds noted the divine authority behind His words. He affirmed, "The words I speak are not My own, but the words of Him who sent Me. His words are true. If a man is thirsty let him come to Me and drink." Such brashness astonished nearly everyone, especially since Jesus had not studied under the supervision of any of the leading teachers of the day. Many of the common people recognized and acknowledged this authority. Even the temple guards whom the scribes sent to arrest Jesus came back without Him. They reported, **"No one ever spoke the way this man does!"**

Last, but certainly not least of all, they faced the problem of fear. What if Jesus continued on His apparent course and began to establish His Messianic kingdom in Israel? What if the Roman legions invaded in response and destroyed the nation and its temple? What if the scribes and Pharisees lost their system, their prestige, their position of honor, and even their lives in the process? Fears like these fueled their violent rejection of Jesus' Messianic claims.

We may deplore the stubborn unbelief that kept the temple leaders from seeing Jesus' true identity. Yet how often in our own lives do we allow pride, the sinful fears of our own flesh, or our faulty human reasoning to blind us to the truth of Jesus' claims on us?

In today's class session you will work with your students to identify particular sins of blindness. It's important that both specific Law and specific Gospel are proclaimed during this class session. Until the students confront their own personal unbelief and stubborn unwillingness to submit to the authority of Jesus as the Christ, they cannot receive from God the power of the Holy Spirit to overcome these sins and to live in the freedom that Christ offers to His people.

Before you continue with your lesson preparation, take a few moments to pray the Holy Spirit's blessing on that preparation. Pray especially that today's lesson touch specific needs of particular individuals in your classes in a meaningful and powerful way.

GETTING INTO THE LESSON (Objective 2)

Use the story of the mayor and the bum given at the beginning of the Student Book material to accent the idea that many times it's difficult to believe good news. The introduction also points out that sometimes believing bad news also presents difficulties for us. Make the point that very often our own feelings and preconceived notions prevent us from confronting truth head-on.

MY MIND IS ALREADY MADE UP
(Objectives 1 and 2)

The references given in the Student Book all contain reasons for the refusal of the scribes and Pharisees to accept the truth that Jesus was the Messiah--the One that God had promised to send. Have the students find each reference and read these aloud in class, discussing them as time permits.

The passage from **John 11:45-53** makes plain the fear behind this refusal. The scribes and Pharisess apparently felt more concern about losing their "place" and their position, than they did about rejecting God's Messiah.

John 12:42-43 indicates the quiet conviction some leaders had that Jesus truly was the Messiah. However, they were apparently unwilling to acknowledge this openly because they feared the social repercussions of such a declaration. Be sure the students recognize the fact that all of us at one time or another are tempted to hide our commitment to Jesus as our Savior. The Pharisees and scribes had fears similar to our own in this respect. We, too, sin as they did and are saved only by the grace of God.

SEEING THE WHOLE TRUTH (Objectives 2 and 3)

The three examples given in this section of the lesson should be recognizable to many students in your class. It may be helpful to group your students in clusters of three or four so everyone has a chance to become involved in the discussion.

Encourage each group to identify the pride, fear, and rebellion that appears to be behind the problems of Laura, Frank, and Marie. Help the students to see that these same sins were responsible for the scribes' and Pharisees' refusal to acknowledge the lordship of Jesus Christ. Use this discussion to help your class begin to identify these kinds of sins in their own lives.

The Student Book suggests that each individual select one of the three students described in this section of the lesson and write a letter to that person sharing a Law/Gospel message. If time permits, let the students begin this exercise in class. Help individuals who seem to need help in focusing the letters they are writing.

Be sure to collect the students' notebooks sometime soon so you can read and comment on the letters they have written. Check for both a Law and Gospel accent in these letters.

Reading assignment for next time: John 8:1-11

Session 19: Authority to Forgive Sins

BIBLE BASIS: John 8:1-11

CENTRAL TRUTH

We humans tend to point out the sins of others as we loudly proclaim our own innocence by comparison. But when we confess our sins, God faithfully forgives our sins and cleanses us from all unrighteousness.

OBJECTIVES

That the students will:
1. Describe the self-righteousness within their own hearts and tell how this sin damages their relationship with God
2. Explain the difference between a Law-oriented and a Gospel-oriented relationship with God
3. Trust joyfully that God forgives them for Jesus' sake
4. Freely forgive others, as they receive power from the Holy Spirit

BACKGROUND

"I didn't do it!"
"He did it too!"
"She did it first!"
"What's so wrong with it? Can't I do as I please?"
"It's not my fault. Talk to those other guys!"

Whether we listen to children argue on a playground, to a conversation between high-school students and their principal, or to adult office or factory workers locked in confrontation with their supervisor, we're likely to hear the same kinds of words--if we will only stick around long enough.

We all make mistakes. We all sin. And we all, on occasion, try to fix the blame for our mistakes and sins on others rather than bearing the responsibility ourselves. We would like to deny personal responsibility for our wrongdoing. We would like to think that others are to blame for our sins. We want to believe that if everyone would become just like us, the world would be a happier place. We need only examine our own attitudes to discover that self-righteousness didn't die with the Pharisees.

Today's narrative from **John 8** exposes the tendency of each human heart to blame others and to judge ourselves righteous in comparison with them. As you study the text for yourself and as you discuss it with your class, it's important to recognize that no one makes a deliberate decision to be pharisaical. No one intends to live in hypocritical self-righteousness. Yet, even sincere Christians can fall into this sin. In fact, those who sincerely want to please God may be more susceptible to this particular fault than others. In our zeal to obey, in our wish to honor God, we may forget that in our weakness we <u>cannot</u> obey. We can do nothing good apart from God's grace working in us. Soon, we may begin to see others as less zealous and thus as less pleasing to God than we ourselves.

Of course, all Christians want to grow stronger in our love for our Father and more and more Christlike in our character. These are truly godly desires. But we dare never forget that all of God's children stand forgiven and acceptable before Him for the same reason--we have been washed in the blood of the Lamb and have been given the free gift of eternal life by God's unimaginable grace. Even the desire to do God's will must come from His Spirit working in our hearts. Not by works of righteousness that we have done or could ever do, but by His grace alone we stand cleansed, forgiven, justified, and empowered to live in a way that reflects His glory and love.

How wonderfully comforting it is to know that God will forgive even the sins of self-righteousness and will replace our pride with humility and love. We need only ask.

Pray as you prepare this lesson that God will lead both you and your class to a thoroughly Gospel-oriented relationship with Him.

GETTING INTO THE LESSON

Use the introductory materials in the Student Book to introduce the concept of guilt and blaming others for our failures. Have the students complete the continuum exercise and talk about why we sometimes find it hard to admit when we're wrong. Read through the excuses and discuss which ones your students have heard and perhaps even used themselves in the past.

CAUGHT IN THE ACT (Objectives 1 and 2)

The Student Book suggests that the students listen carefully while you read **John 8:1-11** aloud. Encourage them to put themselves in the place of the woman who was caught in adultery and brought to Jesus. After they have heard the account, discuss briefly what her feelings may have been.

The questions in the rest of this section deal with the account itself and with the self-righteousness of the scribes and Pharisees.

In discussing question 2, point out that we do not know what Jesus wrote in the dust on the ground. Some have speculated that the Savior wrote names in the dust--names the woman's accusers would recognize as people with whom they had been involved in the same sin as she! While we do not know this to be true, we do know that each of the men present left, apparently feeling some guilt of their own.

As you discuss question 3, deal with the issue of whether forgiveness is "too easy." Does God's promise to forgive all our sins by His grace, for Jesus' sake, lead to a careless attitude toward sin? Refer students to **Rom. 6:1-4** in this connection.

Question 4 provides an opportunity for you to introduce to your students the difference between a Law-oriented approach to righteousness and a Gospel-oriented approach to our relationship with God. Explain this difference and question the students about it to be sure they grasp the distinction.

GUILT, GRACE, JUSTICE (Objectives 1, 2, 3, and 4)

The first two paragraphs in this section will provide an opportunity for you to apply the concepts of grace and justice to specific situations. It may be helpful to students if you take time to roleplay the student council/principal/cheater situation. Of course, the point is that God always forgives. However, we sometimes must face the earthly consequences for our actions. This does not mean that God has not forgiven us, but that for the good of the society in which we live, wrong must be punished. Use the Bible verses listed under the first paragraph to emphasize God's full forgiveness and our response: a forgiving heart, a merciful attitude toward others.

Question 3 in this section asks the students to write a definition explaining the difference between Law and Gospel in our relationship with God. Read through the students' responses as soon after class as possible. Look specifically for legalism in their understanding and speak with individual students for whom this seems to be a problem.

Reading assignment for next time: John 8:12-30

Session 20: Following the Light of Jesus

BIBLE BASIS: John 8:12-30

CENTRAL TRUTH

Jesus is the Light of the world. Whoever follows Him by faith, will not walk in darkness but will have the light of life, just as He has promised.

OBJECTIVES

That the students will:

1. Relate what Jesus meant when He claimed to be the Light
2. Explain the various connotations associated with the Greek word <u>akolouthein</u>--"to follow"--and apply each connotation to their own lives of faith
3. Identify ways the light of Jesus works in their lives--by exposing their sin, assuring them of

God's forgiveness, and empowering them for obedience

BACKGROUND

If we keep in mind that the events of **John 8** took place in Jerusalem during the Feast of Tabernacles, Jesus' words in **verses 12-30** take on even greater significance than may be apparent at first.

On the first day of this particular feast, the "Illumination of the Temple" took place in the Court of the Women. The crowds could watch the festivities which included much joyful dancing and the singing of psalms. Four large candelabra illumined the entire courtyard. This festival provided the dramatic setting for Jesus' bold announcement, "I am the Light of the world. Whoever follows Me will never walk in darkness, but will have the light of life" (v. 12). Passages like **Is. 49:6; 60:1-3**; and several other Old Testament prophecies make it clear that by claiming to be the "Light of the world," Jesus claimed to be the promised Messiah.

Jesus, the Light, dispels the ignorance, superstition, and bondage of sin. As you teach today, you want to aim at helping students use this truth to illumine the dark places of their hearts. You know your class and their particular needs. Look for specific, practical ways to apply the lesson truths to their lives.

GETTING INTO THE LESSON (Objective 1)

Before asking students to look at their Student Book materials, explain to your class the setting for today's text. Ask the students to imagine the events described in **John 8:12-30**. Explain to them the basic outline of the celebration that took place at the Feast of Tabernacles, and also ask someone to read **Deut. 19:15**, to which Jesus refers in the text. Explain this point of Jewish law as necessary. Point out that in this passage the Lord claims His heavenly Father as the second witness to His claim of Messiahship.

Then ask individual students to present a dramatic reading of today's text to the class. You will need someone to assume the role of Jesus. You will also need someone to play these parts:
   A Pharisee
   A group of Pharisees
   A narrator

Allow a few minutes for the actors to skim the text for themselves and then ask them to read it aloud for the rest of the class. As time permits, you may want to repeat the dramatic reading with a different set of actors two or three times to allow more students to participate. Encourage all readers to use as much dramatic expression as possible in portraying this powerful incident.

Then have students turn to session 20 and read through the introductory material about darkness and light.

LET THERE BE LIGHT! (Objectives 1 and 3)

This section of the lesson asks students to use a concordance and other reference materials to find passages that use the word light. Encourage them to consult both the Old and New Testaments. Let the students work on this project individually, using the concordance in the back of their Bible. Or ask them to work with a partner. (Be sure that, in the verses they select, light refers to illumination rather than to the idea of comparative weight.)

After students have had sufficient time to find five or more passages, ask them to choose one as their favorite. Follow the directions given in the Student Book for sharing these with one another. Encourage the students to be as specific as possible when they share their verse and the reason they selected it. If they can refer to a specific, recent incident in their own lives as they speak, this would be ideal.

The second part of this section deals with the darkness of sin. The three passages referenced here explain the working of light in our individual lives as God's people.

Ps. 119:129-130 emphasizes the idea that God's Word enters our hearts to shine light into the dark places there. The light in this sense reveals our sin and our need for the Savior's forgiveness.

1 John 1:5-7 emphasizes the truth that Jesus' blood continually cleanses us from sin as we walk in the light of faith in Him as our Substitute.

Ps. 89:15-17 stresses the point that as we walk in the light of God's presence, He fills our hearts with rejoicing. He shares His glory with us, and He gives us His strength to be able to obey Him, to be able to follow more and more closely the Light of life—our Lord Jesus.

FOLLOW ME! (Objectives 2 and 3)

This section may be assigned as homework if you do not have sufficient time to finish all parts of the lesson in class. The exercise develops various meanings for the Greek term <u>to follow</u> and will be useful in helping your students expand their concept of what it means to live in a day by day personal relationship with the Lord Jesus. The directions in the Student Book should be self-explanatory.

SCATTERING THE DARKNESS (Objective 3)

The assignment given in this part of the Student Book will help the students personalize the message of today's text still further. The directions require students to think and write a prayer asking for increased light in their own lives and hearts. This may in some cases refer to help with particular sins. In other cases, students may be involved in seeking God's peace and hope for situations in their lives that appear dark and hopeless. As the students work, you may wish to play some contemporary Christian music, if this kind of resource is available in your school. In any case, keep the classroom atmosphere quiet, reflective, and devotional.

Reading assignment for next time: John 8:31-59

Session 21: Freedom!

BIBLE BASIS: John 8:31-59

CENTRAL TRUTH

Jesus is the Way, the Truth, and the Life. Faith in Him frees us from slavery to any person, idea, habit, or idol.

OBJECTIVES

That the students will:

1. Describe how unbelievers live in constant, involuntary slavery to sin and how even Christians can be enslaved by sin if they voluntarily submit to it
2. Describe the true freedom from sin's slavery that Jesus won for them by His life, death, and resurrection
3. Tap into the powerful grace of God to break sin's bondages in their lives
4. Celebrate their freedom from sin

BACKGROUND

Session 21 continues a discussion of the confrontation between Jesus and the religious leaders of His time. The words "freedom," "slavery," and "Abraham" always gained the attention of a Jewish crowd. Jesus challenged the nationalistic pride of Israel by suggesting that they were still enslaved by sin, controlled by their own passions and worldly desires. The Savior proclaimed that their Jewish ancestry and heritage did not and could not save them. In what must have appeared to the scribes and Pharisees to be the last straw, Jesus tells them that because of their unbelief, they are actually serving Satan—not the God of their ancestor, Abraham! In angry self-defense, they suggest that Jesus is possessed by a demon. At this point, the Lord declares Himself God's representative. In fact, He claims to be God Himself— I AM **(v. 58)**! All pretense of reason ceases as the crowd picks up stones to hurl at the Savior for His "blasphemy."

No one in Jesus' time wanted to think of himself or herself as enslaved. Still today we would all like to believe ourselves free. No one likes to think of being controlled by any person, desire, or habit. We would all like to believe that we are free! Teenagers especially, as they begin to discover the possibilities of individuality, freedom, and self-identity, want to be free. Yet, many young people serve the god of conformity. Friends, chemicals, clothes, language, and even grades can enslave and cause frustration.

Today's lesson challenges your students to confront the slavery to sin in every area of their own lives. It encourages the students to confess this slavery and to appropriate more fully the freedom Christ has already given them, freedom from sin, death, and Satan.

Read the lesson plan in this guide for session 22 before you teach this session. The two lessons are integrally related in theme and application. The difference lies in the metaphors Jesus used. Decide how best to handle the discussion and worship parts of both sessions so this unity will be most apparent and useful to your students.

GETTING INTO THE LESSON (Objectives 1 and 2)

Read the story of "Box" Jones' escape and discuss the questions that follow. Use the questions about freedom and slavery to stimulate the students' thought processes. Don't attempt to arrive at definite answers at this point in the lesson. You may want to return to these thoughts at the close of the class session if time permits.

CASE STUDIES IN SLAVERY (Objectives 1, 2, and 3)

Let the students read all four of the stories, one at a time. As they do, work through the concepts of freedom and slavery in the lives of each person described. The slavery involved in the life-style each follows should be apparent to all of your students. It is probably more likely that they will be caught up in the slavery of peer pressure than in concerns about financial need or substance abuse. However, you may have students in class that confront any of the four difficulties described.

I'M NOT A SLAVE! (Objectives 1, 2, and 3)

As you work through this section of the lesson, you will want to help the students apply Jesus' words from **John 8:31-59** to the stories from the previous section. The Student Book material also suggests that students read portions of **Rom. 6** and **8**. All three Scripture readings compare slavery to sin with slavery to a human master. Work through the questions in this section together.

Be sure the class understands two kinds of slavery to sin. People who are not Christians, who do not have a living, personal relationship with the Lord Jesus Christ as Savior and Lord, do not experience freedom from sin's power. In fact, they cannot. The Scripture makes clear that original sin so corrupts our nature that we are by nature spiritually blind, dead, and enemies of God.

The second kind of slavery to sin involves those Christians who have received the new birth in Jesus Christ, but who continue to go on living as though that new birth had not occurred. Such a person continues to submit to Satan and his/her own flesh rather than following Christ in obedience and power. Such a life is a life of slavery. Not that any of God's children will live perfect lives here on earth, but we have received power through the grace of God to overcome the sin that wants to keep us in bondage. The Holy Spirit works in our lives to deliver that power to us through the Word and Sacraments. As we use the resources God has made available to us, we become more and more like the Lord Jesus in the things that we speak, think, and do day by day.

The last exercise in this section requires students to choose a person who is a Christian but who seems to be living as a slave to some kind of sin. Depending on your students and the degree of rapport you feel with them, it would be most helpful if you could encourage them to use themselves

as the example. Have them select an area in their life in which they feel themselves to be still under the bondage of sin and/or Satan. They are to identify definite steps they can take to overcome the bondage enslaving them. This exercise will enable you to diagnose which students still live under the Law when they think of the process of sanctification in their lives. A truly Biblical, truly Gospel-centered response to this question will involve:
1. Repentance by God's grace
2. Confession of sin
3. Asking God for the power to live a more Christlike life

Students' responses should also reflect the fact that God works through His Word. Using that Word will be one of our most powerful weapons as we fight the power of sin. You should also briefly mention the Sacraments and the power available to God's people in each.

LET'S WORSHIP! (Objective 4)

As we face both our own sin and the damage that it does in our lives and then as we look at the unique and wonderful power that God gives us to overcome this bondage, we can only respond in awe, love, and worship. The last part of the lesson provides an opportunity for your students to do just that. The Student Book makes several suggestions. Choose the ideas that will work best with your class in the time available. If time does not permit students to work through one of the worship assignments, you may assign one of them as homework. Check session 22 for the worship response suggested there. You may want to assign parts of that session as homework instead.

Reading assignment for next time: John 9

Session 22: Now I See!

BIBLE BASIS: John 9

CENTRAL TRUTH

Jesus is the Light of the world. Faith in Him heals our spiritual blindness and empowers us to walk in the light of His love and truth.

OBJECTIVES

That the students will:
1. Describe how unbelievers live in constant involuntary blindness and how even Christians can be blinded by sin if they voluntarily allow that to happen
2. Describe how once they were blind but now, by God's unimaginable grace, they see—they have been granted spiritual sight
3. Use the light Jesus brings to break the darkness of sin in their lives
4. Celebrate their spiritual sight

BACKGROUND

"One thing I do know. I was blind but now I see!"

Once we were slaves; now we are free! Once we were "nobodies;" now we are the people of God! Once we had not received mercy; now we have received mercy! Once we were without hope and without God in this world. But now! Now we are God's very own children!

The theme of release from slavery, freedom from blindness, deliverance from eternal death began in session 21. We continue this "deliverance" theme in session 22. This time, the metaphor Scripture uses involves not bondage, but blindness.

Jesus came to give sight to the blind. In **John 9**, He does this in a literal way by healing the man born blind. In the subsequent discussion with the scribes and Pharisees about His "crime" of healing on the Sabbath, Jesus extends His miracle to illustrate the distinction between spiritual blindness and spiritual sight. An angry confrontation results between the man who had been healed and the scribes and Pharisees. Ultimately the conflict involves the Lord Himself. Jesus tells the religious leaders of His day that they are the ones who are truly blind. In their stubborn refusal to see the truth about Him as the Messiah, they have chosen to remain in their spiritual blindness.

In this episode, we see both the compassion and judgment of our God. In compassion Jesus reaches out, touches the blind man's eyes, and heals him. The Lord later finds the man and shares with him the Good News that the Messiah has come. In judgment, Jesus confronts the scribes and Pharisees with their obstinate rejection of Him as Messiah. Ultimately He says to them, "If you were blind, you would not be guilty of sin. But now that you claim that you can see, your guilt remains."

In today's session, you will want to point out the similarities in theme between this lesson and the previous one. Share with your students the fact that while the metaphor Scripture uses has changed, the idea of sin/repentance/forgiveness/sanctification remains the same.

Note that the Student Book material included for this particular session involves a chancel drama your class can use in a response of confession and worship. You may wish to incorporate this into a class chapel presentation for your entire school.

GETTING INTO THE LESSON (Objectives 1 and 2)

Ask the students to recall some of the themes that seem to recur in John's gospel. Have them look back through the lessons they have studied to find some of these. For example, they might mention the concepts <u>Word, truth, believe, light, darkness, water, life, glory,</u> and <u>bread</u>. (Other answers are also possible.) Place a list of these words on the chalkboard or a large piece of poster paper. Have students summarize briefly the importance of each theme in Jesus' teachings.

As you list the word <u>light</u>, circle it and have the class recall what they have already learned about this word and its significance in John's gospel. In the course of this discussion, you will want to refer students back to these texts: **John 1:6-9; 3:19-21;** and **8:12.**

If your class did well with the dramatic reading several days ago, you might want to use this method to review the events recorded in **John 9** with the class. You will need a narrator, Jesus, the blind man, neighbors and friends, the scribes and Pharisees, and the blind man's parents. Be sure each person knows which verses he/she will read before you begin the presentation.

DISCUSSING THE ACCOUNT (Objectives 1, 2, and 3)

Use the following questions to guide your students in thinking about the account and its meaning for their lives.

1. In the account from **John 8** we discussed in the last session, Jesus confronted the scribes and Pharisees with their slavery to sin. In **John 9** He quite pointedly accuses them of deliberate spiritual blindness. These were both really calls to repentance. How did the scribes and Pharisees respond? Why was this? Have you ever responded negatively to a call to repent? Why? What is the ultimate result if we continue in this kind of stubborn refusal? **(See v. 41.)**

2. Are slavery to sin and spiritual blindness different names for the same problem? Explain your reasoning. Go back to the four people described in session 21 as enslaved to sin. In what sense are they all spiritually blind as well as enslaved? What truth is "out of sight" for each?

3. Jesus said, "While I am in the world, I am the Light of the world" **(John 9:5).** Jesus also said, "If the Son sets you free, you will be free indeed" **(John 8:36).** What offer is the Savior making in both these statements? What do these statements have to say to those who do not yet know Jesus as their Savior? What do these statements have to say to those who already are Christians?

4. Take the role of the man born blind in **John 9.** Tell what your

thoughts and feelings would be at these points in the story:

verses 1-2; verses 6-7a; verse 7b; verses 8-12; verse 17; verses 24-25; verses 26-34; and verses 35-38.

5. In **verse 38**, John says that the man who had been healed responded in two ways. What were those two ways? How do you suppose his response differed from the "faith" and "worship" of the scribes and Pharisees? (See **John 4:23-24** and **James 2:19**.)

A WORSHIP RESPONSE (Objective 4)

Use part of your session time today as an opportunity for the students to respond in worship to God's love. The Student Book materials for today contains one possible response. You may wish to select a hymn or Scripture song to be sung at the conclusion of each "Failing" section of the chancel drama. Several melodies may be used for the hymn printed in the Student Book. (See LW 43, 45, 344, 494, etc.)

Talk with the students about ways you might use the chancel drama as part of a worship experience in which your class leads the rest of the school during chapel services. The students may suggest hymns that would be appropriate before and after the chancel drama and perhaps also as response verses (see above).

You may also wish to write your own additional "Failing" segments. Emphasize the purpose of the chancel drama--to call the students in your school to repent for times they have acted with deliberate blindness and to assure one another of God's forgiveness in Christ. You also want to give everyone present in the worship service an opportunity to respond in thanksgiving and praise to God for His great goodness and compassion toward us in granting us this forgiveness.

If it is not possible for your students to lead the school in a worship service of this nature, plan a worship experience that can be used in your classroom instead.

As you plan the worship service, you may be aware of contemporary Christian songs written around the themes of light, seeing, blindness, slavery, and freedom in Christ. If this is the case, you may wish to use such music at an appropriate place in the chancel drama itself or before and after the chancel drama is presented. Because these themes are so commonly chosen as the basis for Christian hymns and songs, you may be able to find some very appropriate selections for this purpose.

Reading assignment for next time: John 10

Session 23: I Am the Good Shepherd

BIBLE BASIS: John 10

CENTRAL TRUTH

Jesus is the Good Shepherd. He gathers, feeds, protects and defends those who believe in Him. Those who trust in Him are empowered by the Holy Spirit to listen to Him and follow His loving direction.

OBJECTIVES

That the students will:
1. Explain the metaphor Jesus uses of Himself as the Good Shepherd and themselves as His sheep
2. Identify ways Jesus acts as their Good Shepherd in their daily lives
3. Trust Jesus' protection and care no matter what circumstances they face

BACKGROUND

The metaphor Scripture uses of the Lord as our Shepherd is one of the Bible's most beautiful, serene, and comforting pictures. Because the occupation of shepherd was so common in Bible times, it provided a clear analogy then to which most people could relate. Today, many believers find themselves very far removed from this rural, pastoral culture. We need to study the comparison at some length to derive all the spiritual insights inherent in the metaphor.

Several books will provide additional insight for you and your students as you attempt to broaden your understanding of Jesus' words, "I am the Good Shepherd." You may wish to consult A Shepherd Looks at Psalm 23 by W. Phillip Keller (Grand Rapids: Zondervan, 1970); Home Life in Bible Times by Arthur W. Klinck (St. Louis: CPH, 1947); and/or various Bible dictionaries, encyclopedias, and commentaries.

In **John 10** Jesus also proclaims Himself to be the "Door of the sheepfold." The shepherd of Jesus' time would sleep across the opening to the sheepfold each night. The enclosure had no other entrance. By lying there, the shepherd actually became the "gate." He protected the lambs and the sheep from marauding animals and from thieves. When the sheep left the fold at dawn, the shepherd stood at the gate counting and watching for special needs any sheep might have. He looked to see if any one was sick or hurt. At night when the flock returned, the shepherd counted again. He called individual sheep by name, and he noted which ones needed medicine, salve, or other attention.

Ps. 121:8 promises that God will protect our **"going out and [our] coming in" (RSV).** The phrase in Hebrew suggests that great security can be ours because we can expect and experience God's strong defense in our lives. Our Shepherd knows our goings and comings. He watches over us to meet our individual needs. He calls us by name and even carries us when the path is rough or the road is too long for us.

As you teach this session, your goal will be to enable the young believers in your class to hear and recognize more clearly the voice of Jesus, their Shepherd. And you will want to help them, by the power of the Holy Spirit, to grow in their trust that He calls them by name, cares for them individually, and assumes responsibility for their welfare.

GETTING INTO THE LESSON (Objective 1)
The introductory material in the Student Book describes the life of a typical shepherd in the Holy Land at the time of Jesus. The material is written in the first person. This should make it easier for your students to identify with the feelings and emotions of the shepherd who is describing his work.

Have a student read this introductory section aloud in class. If you were able to obtain reference books giving further, more detailed information about this occupation, spend some time in class right now sharing information about sheep and shepherds with your students. Or assign specific research questions to them and have them use the reference materials to answer the questions.

THE SHEEP AND THE SHEPHERD
(Objectives 1 and 2)
Have the students select a partner and do this activity with their partner. After everyone has jotted down a number of similiarities and differences between Jesus our Good Shepherd and human shepherds, ask the partner pairs to share this information with the whole class. Write their answers on a chalkboard or on a large piece of poster paper. Be sure everyone can read the lists. As you work through this exercise, continue to relate Jesus' care for us today as "His people, the sheep of His pasture."

As time permits, extend this discussion to include a reference to the shepherds God has placed over us in His church--our pastor(s). Talk about the responsibility and the privilege pastors have in taking care of the people of God as undershepherds. Refer the class to such texts as **1 Peter 5:1-4**. (Note: This might be a good time to check your students' ability to use the cross references in their Bible. Ask them to find other references dealing with the same topic in the New Testament, as time permits.)

The last part of this section lists a number of Scripture verses expanding on the theme of Lord as our Shepherd. Have the students follow the directions given in their Student

45

Books. Assign a specific number of references that you wish them to read: two, three, four, or all five.

THE LORD IS MY _____ (Objective 3)

This section asks individuals to write a contemporary paraphrase of either **Ps. 23** or **John 10**. If your students work well together, you may wish them to work together on this assignment. Directions are given in the Student Book. Help individual students as necessary while the entire class works independently on the project. Any students who do not finish in class should take the assignment home to be finished there.

As you grade these paraphrases, keep in mind that the thinking and writing ability of your students will vary greatly. Evaluate each students' work based upon that student's ability rather than upon a comparison with his/her fellow students' work.

Reading assignment for next time: John 11:1-44

Session 24: The Resurrection Connection

BIBLE BASIS: John 11:1-44

CENTRAL TRUTH

Jesus is the Resurrection and the Life. Whoever believes in Him has eternal life, even if he/she dies physically. By His grace, God grants the believer an earthly life of forgiveness, peace, and joy. And He promises us a life with Him in the heavenly home that will never end.

OBJECTIVES

That the students will:

1. Describe Jesus as the Life-Giver sent by God to reveal God's love, His compassion, and His power to deliver us from all our enemies

2. Describe the connection between Lazarus' resurrection, Jesus' resurrection, their own Baptisms, and the final resurrection of all believers

3. Find meaning and purpose in their life as God has created and recreated it in Jesus

BACKGROUND

So often we convince ourselves that Biblical characters were somehow different from us. We picture Mary, Martha, and Lazarus as having perfect faith. And so, of course, Jesus did miraculous things for them. But His power and His willingness to act on the behalf of His friends often seems far removed in both time and space from us and our situation today.

The problem with this view lies in the fact that Biblical characters were imperfect human beings too, just as we are. They faced the same doubts and fears that so often plague us. The Holy Spirit very carefully selected characters and incidents that illustrate this for us, for our comfort and encouragement.

Imagine yourself, for instance, as Lazarus. You have seen your Friend Jesus heal dozens, perhaps even hundreds, of people. You have seen His compassion for the crowds. You have heard Him teach the multitudes about the Father's faithfulness. Then, suddenly, you lie sick--so sick, in fact, that the illness looks as though it may culminate in death. Your sisters, Mary and Martha, send for the Master. As the three of you wait anxiously, the physicians begin to give up. "There's nothing we can do," they say, shaking their heads. Still Jesus does not come. One day. Two days. Still He delays.

Suppose you were Lazarus. How would you feel? Suppose you were Mary or Martha watching helplessly. Suppose you lived next door to this family. You know they have such a strong friendship with Jesus that He often comes to their house for meals. Yet, as His friend Lazarus slips into death, Jesus seems to ignore the urgent request that He come and help.

We don't know what Lazarus, Mary, or Martha were thinking. But we do know what some of the neighbors said: **"Could not He who opened the eyes of the blind man have kept this man from dying" (John 11:37)?** Surely this question ran through Mary's mind, through Martha's thoughts. Later on, when Jesus did come, both sisters said to Him, **"If You had been here, our brother would not have died."**

Thank God that His willingness to help does not depend on our faithfulness, but on His great grace and concern for us! Mary and Martha were right. If Jesus had been there, Lazarus probably would not have died. And God would not have been glorified in the tremendous way that He was as the Lord of life raised His friend.

A few weeks later Jesus glorified God in His own death and resurrection. The Savior defeated sin, death, Satan, and hell forever as He died and rose again for each of us.

Centuries later, death and resurrection continue to glorify God as His people experience death and receive new life in Holy Baptism. We have been buried with Jesus by our baptism into His death. In this Sacrament He gives us new life—eternal life—the life that will never die. We glorify Him as we rely more and more firmly on His grace at work on our behalf in all our circumstances, as we cling to His promises to us in our baptism.

As you work through this lesson, pray for wisdom to communicate these truths more clearly to your students. Pray that the individuals you teach may grow in trust that God is working even in seemingly hopeless circumstances. He will not let them down. (**"Those who hope in Me will not be disappointed"** Is. 49:23.) Pray also that they grow in their desire that God receive great glory from every aspect of every situation in their lives.

GETTING INTO THE LESSON (Objective 1)

The first section of the Student Book raises some questions for the students about the feelings and facts behind today's Bible narrative from **John 11**. It may be helpful to have someone read the narrative directly from John's gospel first as a review. Then work through the introductory material from the Student Book, paragraph by paragraph. Place special emphasis on questions that must have come into the minds of Lazarus, Mary, Martha, and their friends and neighbors in Bethany. Try to elicit from the students questions from their own lives that parallel the questions raised by the Bible narrative.

Keep in mind that you need not (and probably will not) have answers to everyone's questions. All of us at times wonder about God's work in our lives. We wonder about His timing as we await answers to prayer. In our sinfulness, we sometimes question His wisdom. It's important for our students to see that all Christians struggle with these issues at times. Yet God's Word is clear—our Father loves us! Our Savior has authority over life and death. We can trust Him with these all-important issues in our lives.

Begin at this time to emphasize the idea that we can fall back on God's Word, God's promises, and our baptism when doubts begin to creep in along the edges of our minds. We are the children of God, despite our questions, doubts, worries, and fears.

Do not spend a great deal of time at this point with these issues and questions. You will return to them later on in the period.

DATELINE: BETHANY (Objectives 1 and 2)

Let the students look through this material on their own. Then answer the questions briefly in class together.

Then work into the list of interview questions the students will write for the second part of this section in their books. These questions will form the basis of a real press conference you will want to hold in class. Select certain students to play the parts of the people mentioned in the Student Book. Depending on the needs of your class, you may wish to coach each individual beforehand so that that person understands the point of view from which his/her character would speak.

WHAT DOES THIS MEAN? (Objectives 2 and 3)

Your discussion from early in the

class period, together with the truths that surfaced during the class "press conference," should provide a good basis from which students can determine the central truth of this Bible narrative. We want to use this section to help students identify exactly what this narrative means for them. As the students work independently, move around the class giving help to individuals as necessary. Some questions may still remain from the discussion early in the class period. Deal with these as time permits today and if necessary schedule some class time tomorrow.

NOTE: Session 25 will be a review and evaluation activity. Ask your students to go back over the narrative material from the Gospel of John itself that you covered in this unit, the key words from the unit, and the notebook material they have written. Also ask them to have their notebooks in order for next time so that you can evaluate the notebooks while they complete the test.

Session 25: Concluding Activities for Unit 2

See Session 11 for comments regarding possible evaluation activities. Be sure to collect their notebooks and include these as a part of your total evaluation of student work for the unit.

MULTIPLE CHOICE QUESTIONS

1. The word <u>Messiah</u> means (a) God's Son (b) truth (c) God's promised Anointed One (d) almighty **(c)**
2. The Sabbath was (a) a day of worship and rest (b) a rule about special sacrifices (c) a place where Jesus worshiped (d) the place where Christ died **(a)**
3. Nicodemus' problem was that (a) he was a Pharisee and a very old man (b) he needed to repent and be forgiven (c) he had been high priest (d) Jesus refused to speak with him **(b)**
4. Jesus told the woman at the well (a) she needed to be born again (b) adultery could not be forgiven (c) true worship comes as we worship in spirit and in truth (d) as a rabbi, He could not speak with her **(c)**
5. The Jews considered this man the father of their nation: (a) Moses (b) Jesus (c) Isaiah (d) Abraham **(d)**
6. Jesus was called "Rabbi" because (a) the Jews hated Him (b) He was a teacher (c) some believed that He was possessed by a demon (d) He performed many miracles **(b)**
7. A synagogue was (a) a place of death (b) a place where animals were sacrificed (c) a place of prayer and worship (d) a Jewish leader **(c)**
8. The Good Shepherd (a) feeds us on His Word (b) gives us living water to drink (c) defends us from Satan (d) is Jesus (e) all of the above are correct **(e)**
9. The woman at the well was (a) a Samaritan (b) Mary (c) a Pharisee (d) a Rabbi **(a)**
10. A self-righteous person (a) will never be defeated by Satan (b) is truly humble (c) is lazy (d) does not want to confess sins (e) none of the above are correct **(e)**

TRUE/FALSE QUESTIONS

1. We must feel sorry enough before God will forgive our sins. **(F)**
2. Lazarus had been dead for two days when Jesus arrived. **(F)**
3. To "blaspheme" means to show disrespect for God. **(T)**
4. Dualism is a philosophy that argues that good is much stronger than evil. **(F)**
5. Repentance is a gift from God, not a feeling we work up inside ourselves by trying hard to feel sorry. **(T)**
6. None of Jesus' disciples believed He was the Messiah. **(F)**
7. A disciple is one who follows his/her master and learns from the master. **(T)**
8. The scribes and Pharisees trusted in themselves and their own goodness before God. **(T)**

9. Christ's main purpose in coming to earth was to die on the cross so we could receive forgiveness of sins and eternal life. **(T)**

10. Jesus was both the Son of God and the Son of Man. **(T)**

SHORT ANSWER QUESTIONS

1. What needs do all people have? How has God met each of those needs for you?

2. What does it mean that Jesus is your Good Shepherd? What things does He do for you as your Shepherd?

3. In what two ways is Jesus our Light?

4. In your own words, explain what the Bible means when it says we must be "born again."

5. Give two or three examples of "spiritual blindness" in our world.

Feel free to duplicate the questions above for use in testing. Please add the following credit line: Concordia Publishing House. Copyright 1986.

Unit 3: Bearing Much Fruit

This unit stresses our focus and our priorities as God's people. By His grace, God's Spirit enables us to spend and be spent for God's glory—just as our Savior was. The unit should challenge your students to lose their lives in service to others and thus find true meaning, purpose, and adventure in life. Redeemed and forgiven, we become more and more Christlike as we live "in Him."

PLANNING THE UNIT

Session 36: You will need a supply of 3 x 5 cards for this session.

Session 26: Anointed for the Mission

BIBLE BASIS: John 11:45--12:11

CENTRAL TRUTH

God anointed Jesus, the Messiah, for His special mission—saving all people from their sins. Once we see God's great love in Christ, our hearts overflow with gratitude. We live, empowered by God's Spirit, in an attitude of worship.

OBJECTIVES

That the students will:

1. Describe their personal attitudes about worship, giving, and their purpose in life

2. Define the term <u>parallel passage</u> and be able to find parallel passages for Biblical texts

3. Explain how attitudes led to actions in the lives of Mary, Jesus, Judas, and the Jewish religious leaders of Jesus' day

4. Ask God for attitudes and motives that bring glory to Him and joy to themselves and others

BACKGROUND

"What makes that person tick?" Maybe you've wondered that about a student in your class, a colleague in your school, or a child in your home. We know instinctively that, most of the time, the attitudes behind people's actions motivate individuals to act as they do.

In today's Bible narrative we see Mary, motivated by a heart overflowing with gratitude. We see Judas, motivated by the greed of a thief for whom money had become a god. We see the curious crowds traveling to Bethany to see not only the Miracle-Worker but the man He raised from death. We see the chief priests so consumed by fear that they officially decide to plot the death of an innocent man, the Messiah Himself. And we see Jesus, moving among this cross section of humanity, loving sinners to the absolute maximum.

Love motivated Jesus in all that He did.

As you teach this lesson you will challenge the young Christians in your class to evaluate their motives, the attitudes of their hearts. You want them to see once again the great love of the Savior as He willingly prepares for His "hour" of glory. And you want them to consider that they, too, have been anointed for special service to God in a special way, just as Jesus was. You want your students to take time to reflect on this as they sit at Jesus' feet to ponder the meaning and ultimate purpose of their lives. Pray for the individuals in your class as you continue your preparation for today's session.

GETTING INTO THE LESSON (Objective 1)

Have the students complete the rating scale found at the beginning of this session in their books. Explain the activity for any students who do not understand the printed instructions. This assignment presupposes they have read the Bible section for today. If you did not assign **John 11:45--12:11** at the end of session 25, you will need to give your students time to read through the account before they complete the questionnaire.

Ask individuals to share their opinions, but do not lead the class into an extended discussion at this point. You may wish to come back to these statements for further discussion later on.

AN ATTITUDE OF GRATITUDE (Objectives 2 and 3)

If your students are not familiar with the term parallel passages, explain this concept. The Student Book presupposes that students have access to the cross references and parallel passages for the text in their personal study Bibles. If they do not, you should give them the references for the two parallel texts. These are **Matt. 26:6-13** and **Mark 14:3-9**.

The students should fill out the chart on their own and then compare responses. As they work, encourage more than surface answers. They should try to visualize the events in their minds in a realistic way and report what they probably would have seen and heard had they been invited to the party at Simon's house.

As time permits, discuss the Biblical practice of anointing and its meaning. Refer students to concordances, Bible dictionaries, and/or topical handbooks. Or have them read and discuss **1 Sam. 9:15-16; 10:1; 15:1; Is. 61:1-3; Luke 4:18-19;** and **Acts 10:38**. How was Jesus the "Anointed One"?

The next part of this section in the Student Book deals with the motivation behind each character's actions in this text. Discuss what each of these may have been. The introductory material in this guide may be of some help. You want to stress Mary's gratitude; Judas' greed; Jesus' love; the chief priests' fear and jealousy; and the curiosity of the crowds who came to see both Jesus and Lazarus.

Point out the interesting nature of these responses. Nearly all the characters mentioned had seen nearly the same events and had heard much of the same teaching that the Lord had done. Yet such a disparity existed between the response of each person's heart. Talk about why this might have been.

WHAT MOTIVATES ME? (Objectives 1 and 4)

Have someone in the class read through the paragraphs describing Mary's motivation, Jesus' motivation, and our motivations.

The last paragraph in this section asks the students to write a letter to Jesus. Read through this paragraph aloud and answer questions your students may have about the assignment. You will probably want them to put their letter in their notebooks. Work with individual students as necessary to help them complete the assignment in a meaningful way.

As an extension of this assignment, you might ask students to share some of what they have written with a partner. Take care to do this in such a way that it is not threatening. It would probably be best if the students were allowed to choose their own partners.

As you grade the letters the students have written, look especially for evidence of individuals who seem to be struggling with the issues raised in this lesson. As you read, you may discover opportunities for ministry with individual students. Pray for these individuals, and think about ways you might counsel with them individually or refer them to someone who has expertise in career counseling, etc.

Reading assignment for next time: John 12:12-50

Session 27: Glorify Your Name!

BIBLE BASIS: John 12:12-50

CENTRAL TRUTH

Jesus endured the agony and humiliation of His crucifixion willingly because He could see the outcome--our salvation. Because of this, He joyfully gave His life for us. Now He calls us to use His power to lose our lives for His sake. As we do, we find eternal and significant purpose in our own life and death.

OBJECTIVES

That the students will:
1. Relate that Jesus gave up His life willingly so that He could "draw all men unto Himself"
2. Explain in contemporary terms Jesus' miniparable about the grain of wheat "dying"
3. Express a desire to bring glory to God in their daily lives by repenting of their sins of selfishness and by living lives more and more deliberately focused on serving their Savior and serving others

BACKGROUND

The Christian life is a life of many paradoxes. Today's lesson focuses on one of these. Jesus promises us, **"The man who loves His life will lose it, while the man who hates his life in this world will keep it for eternal life"** (John 12:25).

The Savior not only taught this paradox, He lived it. Throughout the gospel accounts, we see Jesus giving His life away, showing all those around Him what God's love and compassion are really like. How strongly the last week of the Savior's life exemplifies this! As He rode into Jerusalem, Jesus knew what the outcome would be. He foresaw the beatings, the cross, the shame, the pain, and the death that would be His.

Yet, He saw something else as well. **Heb. 12:2** says that Jesus **"for the joy that was set before Him, endured the cross, despising the shame"** (RSV). Perhaps we have never thought much about what was in Jesus' mind as He hung on the cross. But this verse gives us a hint: He thought of us and of our salvation. He thought of having us as His brothers and sisters. He thought of the joy of sharing His gift of eternal life with us. That joy urged Him onward. That joy gave Him the impetus to go through with the agonizing ordeal. He endured the cross for the joy of someday having us home with Him in the Father's house! He knew that when He was lifted up, people of all backgrounds, people of all races, people of all abilities, people of all nations would be drawn to Him. They would "see Jesus"--and seeing Him, by faith receive life, real life, eternal life.

Now, Jesus invites His followers to lose themselves in serving Him and in serving others. This call challenges all believers, but young people may find His call particularly difficult. The world system all around us says we find ourselves by serving ourselves. The world system urges us to seek first our own ease, our own comfort. The world system emphasizes prestige, power, and possessions. As adolescents struggle to establish their own identity and to refine their purpose in life, the values the world system pushes seem very attractive.

51

As you teach, keep in mind that Jesus never tried to argue the truth of His teaching. He never tried to prove the paradox. He told the scribes and Pharisees, **"If anyone chooses to do God's will, he will find out whether My teaching comes from God or whether I speak on My own"** (John 7:17).

To find our lives we must lose them. The paradox makes no logical sense. And yet, as the Savior said, when we act on His teaching, we find that it works.

Pray for wisdom to communicate the truth of this paradox in a powerful way today. Pray that the Holy Spirit will empower the young Christians in your class to see that, by God's grace, as they lose their lives, they will truly find themselves.

GETTING INTO THE LESSON

The first activity has been designed to stimulate students' thinking about their ultimate purpose in life. If many of the students seem familiar with the account from <u>Tom Sawyer</u>, simply read through the information given in the Student Book to refresh their memory. If, however, many seem unfamiliar with this book, you may wish to read parts of the chapter described here to them.

Ask if the kind of "selective memory" the townspeople showed as they thought about Huck, Joe, and Tom occurs at funerals today. Briefly discuss this phenomenon and the reasons behind it.

WHO WILL REMEMBER ME? (Objective 3)

As one variation to the activity in the Student Book, you might give each student a blank sheet of paper. Have them draw a simple tombstone on the page and in 25 words or less write an epitaph for themselves. Ask them to write the epitaph they would like to see appear on their tombstone as a testimony to other people about what their life had been like. As time permits, let the students share their responses with one another and justify their choices.

A MINIPARABLE (Objective 2)

Work through this part of the session together. The parable may be difficult for some students to understand. If necessary, simply explain it yourself.

BRINGING GLORY TO GOD (Objectives 1 and 3)

Have the students skim today's Bible reading once again. Help them see that each event in this section exemplifies Jesus' desire to bring glory and honor to His heavenly Father in everything He did. Students should see Jesus' desire to bring God glory as the unifying theme for this entire section.

Although the rejection by the Jewish leaders is not listed in the Student Book, you may wish to discuss it in terms of how even it brought glory to God. (See **vv. 17-19** and **37-50**.) The Old Testament prophets had foretold that many would reject the Messiah, whom God sent. Even in their rejection, the scribes and Pharisees vindicated God's Word by verifying the ancient prophecies.

Students should be able to use any good topical handbook or concordance to find appropriate passages for the second exercise in this section of the lesson. Among the many appropriate passages in the Scriptures are **1 Cor. 10:31; 2 Cor. 3:18; Eph. 1:12, 14;** and **Phil. 1:9-11**. Highlight **1 Cor. 10:31**, as it so clearly speaks the truth about God's purpose for us in bringing glory to Him.

The passage from **2 Thess.** tells us that God wants to share His glory with us. He does this for us now as He forgives our sins, as He keeps all of His promises to us, and as He continually assures us of His love for us. Ultimately, of course, we will share God's glory when we arrive home in heaven.

Use the last part of this section to help students think about specific actions they can take to bring glory to their heavenly Father. Give them time to go back over the three purpose statements they wrote at the beginning of the lesson (or the epitaphs they composed). Allow them to change any of their statements if they wish to do so at this point. But challenge them to explain the changes they have made.

As the students begin to think about the three specific things they could do to glorify God in their lives today, be sure the discussion includes both Law and Gospel. We do not always glorify God by what we think, say, and do. A recognition of this fact should lead to an attitude of repentance, an attitude of thankfulness to God for His promise of forgiveness, and a desire to serve God and others--thus bringing glory to God. After the students have made their lists, ask them to check their attitudes in these three areas. Our motivation for doing things that please our Father must be one of response to His marvelous grace in Christ our Lord, rather than a desire to earn His favor. Assure the students of God's forgiveness before they leave the classroom today.

Reading assignment for next time: John 13:1-17 and Matt. 20:20-28

Session 28: The Sign of a Servant

Bible Basis: John 13:1-17; Matt. 20:20-28

CENTRAL TRUTH

Jesus Christ, God's Son, emptied Himself and became true man to faithfully carry out His mission as God's Servant. Believers, empowered by God the Holy Spirit, serve others as they follow Jesus' example.

OBJECTIVES

That the students will:
1. Describe the humility and love for sinners they see in Jesus' act of washing the disciples' feet
2. Tell what it means to be a "servant of all"
3. Recognize and repent of past attitudes of selfishness and pride and be assured of God's forgiveness
4. Identify ways they can love and serve others as Jesus has loved and served them

BACKGROUND

How often Jesus surprised His disciples. The things He did and the concepts He taught so often ran counter to commonly accepted human wisdom. Who could imagine a king washing his subjects' feet? Who would have thought the Messiah would stoop to do such a menial task, a task usually reserved for household slaves?

How often Jesus continues to surprise His followers even today. We have received titles like "kings and priests," titles like "God's chosen people," and "sons and daughters of the living God." We have access to the heavenly Father's throne room in prayer. We, who by God's grace have received this greatly privileged position--we, too, have received a servant's role. We, too, have been called to wash feet. A servant is no greater than his (or her) Master.

How often, though, we look for ways to excuse ourselves from this responsibility. Sometimes people who work with teens find ways to excuse the adolescents with whom they work as well. Some adults (and some teens too) still need to be convinced that young people can and should accept some adult responsibility. Some believe adolescence to be a time of justified self-centeredness, self-concern, and self-indulgence.

Yet study after study has shown that most youth are not only able, but feel eager, to live sacrificially. Their idealism can be channeled by the Holy Spirit into an increasing concern for others. Empowered by the Spirit they can truly find themselves by giving themselves, by taking up their cross and following Jesus in humility and joy.

The lessons of servanthood do not come easily at any age. Our young people need to see in us an attitude of compassion. They need to see us model for them the servant's heart. As you challenge the students in your class today, pray that each of them would catch a glimpse of the adventure such a life-style offers. Pray also for continuing growth in humility and the desire to serve God and others in your own life.

GETTING INTO THE LESSON

Begin by asking students why government officials, up to and including the president of the United States or the prime minister of Canada, are called "public servants." Ask them to think of incongruous situations suggested by the "inverted pyramid" style of leadership Jesus describes in **Matt. 20:20-28**. For example, ask them to imagine the speaker of the House of Representatives sitting outside Congress shining the shoes of the tourists who have come to visit Washington, D.C. Or visualize the chairperson of your school's board of education in the locker room after a basketball game picking up smelly sweat socks and taking uniforms home to wash.

Then have the students complete the introductory section from session 28 in their Student Books. This activity is intended to help students begin to recognize the selfishness that sometimes motivates them.

Discuss the choices each person made and the reasons behind those choices. Some students may pick a certain task because it would be easiest or least disgusting to them. Others may choose based on wanting to help a specific, favorite person. Some may choose a job because of the personal recognition it might bring or because it would be exciting (sandbagging, for example).

After everyone has had a chance to contribute, ask if any choices or reasons were selfish. Don't permit anyone to "confess" someone else's sins. Rather, allow a minute or so for individual reflection. Then ask for comments from students about their own choices and their own reasons.

CALLED TO SERVE (Objectives 1 and 2)

Have students work together with a partner to do this research. If not enough Bible dictionaries or encyclopedias are available, have one or two students find the information for which the Student Book asks.

After you have discussed ways people could be enslaved, point out that very few of these ways were voluntary. Slaves became slaves by being taken as prisoners of war; by being given away, perhaps by parents, to pay a debt; by birth if one's parents were already slaves; and as a penalty for theft if the thief had no way to pay for what he/she had stolen. In the Roman world, parents sometimes exposed unwanted infants. Anyone who would find and care for these infants could claim the child as a personal possession.

As students read **Matt. 20:25-28**, tell them that the word, <u>servant</u>, Jesus used here could just as easily be translated <u>bondservant</u> or <u>slave</u>. Have them reread **verses 25-28** aloud, substituting <u>slave</u> for <u>servant</u> if their Bible version uses <u>servant</u>.

Then have **Phil. 2:5-8** read aloud from several different translations. Ask students to paraphrase these verses in their own words. Note that Jesus became a servant (slave) for us voluntarily--because He loved us. He emptied Himself of His rights and power as God and came to earth to serve us and finally to die for us on a cross. Explain briefly that crucifixion represented the most humiliating and painful way anyone in the ancient world could die. That's why Paul explains it in the way he does: **"--even death on a cross!"** He is saying to his readers, "Just think of it! Death by crucifixion!"

IMAGINE THAT! (Objectives 1 and 2)

Read through this section of the lesson together. Explain the writing assignment in more detail as necessary for your students. Then allow 10--15 minutes for students to outline their responses in class. Assign the writing of a final version in their notebooks as homework and let them know your plans for collecting and grading the assignment.

After students have had time to outline their ideas, ask individuals to briefly share some of their thoughts. Point out the self-centeredness and self-justification that must have existed in the disciples' hearts as they thought about lowering themselves to do the work of a lowly household slave. Also draw out the surprise and shock the disciples must have felt when they saw their King, their Lord, tie the towel around Himself and kneel on the floor beside the water basin.

A SLAVE? WHO ME? (Objective 3)
This section should help students think about specific personal attitudes and actions. They should be led to identify areas in their lives that are not modeled after the Servant-King they serve. After students have completed the exercise, ask volunteers to share responses and feelings.

The last sentence-completion exercise provides opportunity to recognize specific sins of pride and selfishness. Allow time for silent confession. Then assure students that, for the sake of Jesus, God does indeed forgive all our sins.

BECOMING A SERVANT (Objective 4)
Explain the servant project described in the last part of this lesson. Have students select a specific project on which they wish to work. Assign a specific date by which they are to tell you what they will do and when it will be completed. Collect and comment on notebooks soon after the projects have been completed.

Reading assignment for next time: John 13:18-30

Session 29: Is It I, Lord?

BIBLE BASIS: John 13:18-30

CENTRAL TRUTH
God's love for us in Christ is so strong that no sin can ever separate us from Him. Even Judas could have found forgiveness had he come to Jesus in repentance and faith.

OBJECTIVES
That the students will:
1. Identify the process by which Satan led Judas into "little sins" and then into "bigger and bigger" ones, until he had trapped Judas in despair and finally destroyed him
2. Identify situations today in which Satan tempts young people into "Judas sins" of unfaithfulness and disloyalty to God and to others
3. Differentiate between regret for sin and true repentance
4. Repent for sins of betrayal and faithlessness and be assured of God's forgiveness in Christ Jesus

BACKGROUND
Judas probably had little idea of what was happening to his heart. Satan works so subtly! And yet, Scripture paints a bleaker picture of no other character. Jesus Himself commented that it would have been better for Judas had he never been born.

Surely when Judas joined the little band of Jesus' followers, he did not intend to become the most infamous traitor of all history. So what happened? What caused such a meteoric fall?

Scripture gives us a few clues. Perhaps when Judas was integrated into the group of Jesus' closest disciples, he showed evidence of business acumen. At any rate, he became treasurer for the group. Maybe he, like the other eleven, looked forward to the day Jesus would declare independence from Roman rule and begin a revolution to overthrow the Gentile army garrisoned in Israel.

It soon became obvious, however, that any hopes Judas had of assuming a high position in Jesus' earthly kingdom would never materialize. In fact, as far as he and the other eleven could see, Jesus' kingdom itself would never materialize. Judas' heart must have filled with disappointment and then with disgust and indignation. He became a thief. His pretended zeal for kingdom principles like helping the poor **(John 12:6)** grew out of a covetous and hypocritic heart.

Apparently, Jesus' other eleven followers trusted Judas to the end. But the Savior knew what was happening inside this disciple's heart. In love, Jesus reached out to Judas again and again. He warned and invited. He called Judas "friend," even after the betrayal. But His overtures fell on sin-deafened ears.

At the last, Judas felt deep regret for his sin. But regret is not repentance. Instead of turning to Jesus for forgiveness and power, he chose to turn away. Judas died in despair--his final sin and the one that damned him.

What has this sad story to do with you and with the young people that sit in your classroom today?

For one thing, it points out the subtlety with which Satan works. Judas's sin began perhaps in self-centeredness. From there it progressed to disappointment--to anger--to greed and petty theft--to hypocrisy--to coveteousness and betrayal--to despair--to suicide. The chain can be configured in a number of ways. The point, though, is that Satan didn't come to Judas with suicidal thoughts--not at first. The attack began much more innocently. It resulted in eternal death.

We should not assume that the enemy's tactics have changed much in the centuries since. He lures us into innocent-looking transgressions with an eye toward enmeshing us inextricably in unbelief and despair when he has finished with us.

The second and the hopeful point involves God's limitless love. Even a Judas could have found the Savior's forgiveness. Had he repented, all his greed, hypocrisy, anger, theft, and even his betrayal itself would have been forgiven. After all, Jesus forgave and restored Peter.

As you teach today, you will want your students to see especially that no sin is ever too big for the limitless love of God. We cannot out-sin His grace. What Good News that truly is!

GETTING INTO THE LESSON
Use the introductory material from the Student Book to introduce the idea that Judas' name will go down in infamy. Work through the questions printed in this section.

WHY, JUDAS? WHY? (Objectives 1 and 3)
The passages listed in this unit provide a comprehensive summary of the New Testament remarks about Judas' character and reputation. Let the students read the references listed and jot down what they discover about this disciple from their reading. Share results of the research by writing notes on the chalkboard or on a large piece of poster paper.

Next, have students read through the letter from Judas. Of course, the paragraphs are speculative. Use this section to begin a discussion about Judas' feelings and character. The questions in the Student Book should provide adequate material for discussion. Consult the **"Background"** material from this lesson for commentary you may wish to share with your students during this discussion.

WHY, KAREN? WHY? (Objectives 2 and 3)
Use this section to zero in on specific temptations the students in your class face today--temptations that resemble those that Judas faced. Have someone read Karen's story from the Student Book aloud. Then discuss the questions that follow. These questions parallel the ones you discussed in the previous section about Judas.

As an alternative to whole-class discussion, you might have the students form small groups of three or four. Ask them to discuss the questions within their groups. Then come together and share insights as a whole class.

DEAR GOD, HELP! (Objectives 2, 3, and 4)
During the last several minutes of the period, allow the students to work on the letter assigned in this section in the Student Book. They are to write the letter in their class notebooks. Make plans to read and comment on their letters as soon as possible.

<u>Reading assignment for next time:</u>
John 13:31-38

Session 30: Love One Another

BIBLE BASIS: John 13:31-38

CENTRAL TRUTH

In self-sacrificial love, Jesus gave Himself for sinners. That kind of love has become the distinguishing mark of Jesus' followers, just as the Savior said it would: **"All men will know that you are My disciples if you love one another."**

OBJECTIVES

That the students will:
1. Think about and evaluate the various kinds of love human beings experience
2. Describe Jesus' death as the supreme act of love, which demonstrated the glory of the Father
3. Describe the Biblical connection between God's love for us and our love for others
4. Evaluate their personal witness of agape love
5. Discover new and creative ways to fulfill Christ's command to "love one another"

BACKGROUND

Young people like to think, sing, and talk about love. As they grow and mature, they anxiously await the experience of love in all its forms. Many, especially those from homes where love has been absent, crave the love of teachers, friends, and coaches. They will do almost anything to receive love from others. Other young people foolishly believe they fully understand love and how it should feel.

Jesus' command sounds simple. But as those who have tried to practice it have found, loving is not as easy as it sounds. To love like Jesus loves involves following Him to Calvary. That kind of love willingly gives all to serve others. It derives its uniqueness and its power from the heart of God Himself. Jesus' hour of glory (the hour of His death) reveals to sinners God's true character: God is love!

True love, God's love, is unknown among the people of the world. It runs contrary to human notions of love, even the most altruistic. God's kind of love does indeed involve our emotions. But God's love is at its heart primarily a commitment, a commitment of self-sacrifice and service. Only God loves fully. Only He can give love in full measure to us. By His grace, we can receive, experience, and share it. We, of ourselves, have no potential to contain or to display the kind of love Jesus showed. But when God's forgiveness and peace flow into our hearts, the Holy Spirit enables us to do the impossible: He enables us to love. By His grace we can love one another as He has loved us.

I LOVE YOU! (Objective 1)

Read the introductory comments in the Student Books about love and its meanings in different contexts. Then let the students work on their lists of love songs. If you assigned this as homework, let volunteers share some of the titles they have listed.

Next, explain to your class four of the most common Greek words for love. You may want students to write these definitions in their notebooks, rather than in the Student Books.

storge--This word includes feelings of affection between people, primarily the kind of affection parents feel for their children. It is also used to describe children's love for parents. Neither storge nor eros appear in the New Testament.

phileo--This kind of love is often described as "brotherly affection." Phileo and agape are the two New Testament words translated "love." Phileo is used in about five percent of the New Testament references to love. It's the kind of love siblings and good friends have for one another. Thus, Philadelphia is the "city of brotherly love."

eros--Eros involves sexual attraction and the kind of passionate love husbands and wives feel for one another. The English word erotic is

57

derived from eros.

agape--The New Testament uses this Greek word for love most often (about 95 percent of the time). The word is almost unknown in pagan or secular literature of the time. It refers to selflessness and self-sacrifice. This love drove Jesus to the cross as our Substitute. More than a feeling, agape represents a decision--a decision to act for the good of another despite the personal cost involved.

After you have defined the four kinds of love, ask students to give specific examples of each.

Note: For further study on your own, you might read The Four Loves by C. S. Lewis (New York: Macmillan, 1960). Lewis takes an in-depth look at each word, what it meant to the Greeks at the time the New Testament was written, and what implications each has for Christians today.

LOVE--IN OTHER WORDS (Objectives 1, 3, and 4)

Use this part of the lesson to probe the selfish ends we humans often have in mind when we use the word love. All three examples given represent selfish, manipulative ways people "love." Ask volunteers to give examples from their own lives of times they have loved conditionally or have been loved conditionally.

Ask whether or not we have to use these exact words to love conditionally. Can we love someone conditionally without saying, "I will love you if . . .," or "I love you because . . ."?

Talk about the lack of security one feels in a relationship based on conditional love. When someone says, "I love you because you're so strong (or beautiful, or athletic)," our minds fill with question marks about what will happen when we no longer live up to the standards our "lover" has set. Use one or more of the following situations to stimulate discussion:

1. E. J. says to Margie, "I love you because you're so beautiful." A few weeks later, Margie is badly burned in a fire in her family's apartment. As she lies in the hospital's intensive care unit, she thinks about her relationship with E. J. What concerns will she have? Are these concerns wellfounded or not?

2. Jari tells Karen, "Our friendship is so great. I'd sure rather stay with you than with Patty while my parents are on vacation. Do you think you could invite me?" What thoughts will cross Karen's mind when Jari says this? Is Jari trying to manipulate Karen? Explain your opinion. Does love always mean we do what the other person wants us to do or asks us to do? Why or why not?

3. Judas loved Jesus. He joined the group of disciples and became their treasurer. Then it became clear Jesus did not intend to set up an earthly kingdom. None of the disciples would assume high positions in Jesus' government. So Judas looked for a way to make a few shekels from their relationship anyway. What kind of love did Judas have for Jesus? What kind of love did Jesus have for Judas? Have you ever known anyone who chose friends based on what he/she could get out of the relationship? Have you ever made friends with someone so you could give in the relationship? Does God expect all our relationships to be giving ones? If they are, how will we ever get our own needs met?

LOVE--NO MATTER WHAT (Objectives 2, 3, 4, and 5)

Review the meaning of agape before the students read the passages from **John** and **1 John**. Have students volunteer specific examples of how Jesus demonstrated the kind of love described in both readings.

The Student Book suggests that students read the verses from **1 Cor.** three times. This should demonstrate the fact that only Jesus has loved perfectly with the kind of love described in these verses. The passage contains both Law and Gospel. Ask students to identify each. (When we compare our own failures to love with the specific description here, we see how far short we fall of God's kind of love. On the other hand, when we read the verses thinking of how very patient, kind, encouraging, and forgiving God is with us--what comfort we feel! His love empowers us to love others--unconditionally.)

To close, ask students to think about the "servant projects" they chose for session 28. Ask volunteers to describe what they have done. Discuss the feelings that accompanied the actions. Did their feelings change as they began to serve the other person(s)? How so? Why does this sometimes happen? Will we ever be able to love completely unconditionally, as Jesus did?

Explain your opinion.

Before dismissing the students, pray 1 Cor. 13:4-8a. As you read through the text, change the words into a request. ("Dear Father, We come to you asking that you would help us love as You love us. Please help us to endure long and to be patient and kind. Keep us from being envious and from boiling over with jealousy . . .")

Reading assignment for next time: John 14:1-14

Session 31: Jesus, the Way to the Father

BIBLE BASIS: John 14:1-14

CENTRAL TRUTH

Jesus alone is the Way, the Truth, and the Life. No one can come to the Father except through Him. By faith in the Savior we are put into a right relationship with God. This relationship gives us peace, a purpose for living, the privilege of prayer, and the promise that God will hear and answer our prayers.

OBJECTIVES

That the students will:
1. Describe Jesus' claim to be the Way, the Truth, and the Life
2. Explain how pride, rebellion, and fear keep us from coming to God in confidence
3. Confess sins of pride, rebellion, and fear in their own lives and be assured of God's forgiveness for Jesus' sake
4. Use the power of prayer, trusting God to answer their prayers for His glory and their own good

BACKGROUND

The exclusive claims of the Gospel offend sinners. As Paul wrote to the Corinthians, **The message of the cross is foolishness to those who are perishing, but to us who are being saved it is the power of God. For it is written: "I will destroy the wisdom of the wise; the intelligence of the intelligent I will frustrate"** (1 Cor. 1:18-19).

Absolute truth does exist and we can know it. Yet this notion is foolishness to most of our contemporaries. "Truth is relative," they intone knowingly.

The idea that the person who comes to God must come by faith in Christ alone is ludicrous to most people of our age. "My god is more inclusive than that," they assert.

The concept that abundant life, true life, eternal life come only through a living, personal relationship with the Lord Jesus causes rebellion and pride to rise in the hearts of most people in our society.

Yet, Jesus made these exact claims--without apology: **I am the Way the Truth and the Life. No one comes to the Father except through Me** (John 14:6).

Paul explains further: **God chose the foolish things of the world to shame the wise; God chose the weak things of the world to shame the strong. He chose the lowly things of this world and the despised things-- and the things that are not--to nullify the things that are, so that no one may boast before Him. It is because of Him that you are in Christ Jesus, who has become for us wisdom from God--that is, our righteousness, holiness, and redemption. Therefore, as it is written: "Let him who boasts, boast in the Lord"** (1 Cor. 1:27-31).

Knowing this in our heart of

59

hearts, trusting it, gives us confidence before God. It's no accident that both Jesus (**John 14:1-14**) and John (**1 John 5:13-15**) link the assurance of our salvation with the powerful privilege of confident prayer. As John writes, **"This is the assurance we have in approaching God . . ."** We can approach God confidently because we know for sure Jesus is the only way to the Father. We know the truth about God, about ourselves, and about God's love for us. We have the gift of life that makes us sons and daughters of the King of kings.

Pray that the young people in your class today grasp more firmly the peace these truths produce in Christian hearts. Pray also that as a result of what happens in this lesson, the students will approach God with even more confidence than they have before, knowing who they are in Christ by His abundant grace.

GETTING INTO THE LESSON

Place the word relativism on the chalkboard. Ask if anyone knows what it means. If necessary, prompt responses by using a sentence or two to describe this philosophy. For example, "Everything is relative," or "It all depends," or "Everyone's entitled to his own opinion. Who's to say you're wrong?"

Then have someone find the word in a dictionary and read the definition. Ask, **Can Christians be relativists? From what you know of the Bible, is "everything relative"?** Urge the students to defend their opinions.

THE WAY, THE TRUTH, THE LIFE
(Objectives 1 and 2)

Have the students listen carefully while you read **John 14:1-14** aloud to them. Tell them that even though they have read this section before class, you want them to listen to the words once more. This time, they should listen as though they believe that everything is relative. What "outrageous" claims does Jesus make in this passage?

List these claims on the chalkboard or on a large piece of poster paper. Then work through the material in the Student Book about Jesus' claim to be the Way, the Truth, and the Life.

After students answer the last question in the section, have them read **Rom. 2:12-13.** God promises to judge those without faith in Jesus. And He always keeps His promises, whether promises of Law or promises of Gospel.

REJECTING THE TRUTH (Objectives 2 and 3)

You may want students to work in small groups to read and summarize the passages listed in this section. The verses all point out the rebellion, pride, and fear that human beings have when they think about God and the demands of His Law.

After you discuss this concept in general as it applies to other people, ask students to apply it to themselves. When do we rebel against God's demands? When does pride keep us from admitting our sin and asking God to forgive and cleanse us?

Reserve a few minutes to talk specifically about ways fear sometimes causes us to reject God's truth. Sometimes we fear that God places limits on His forgiveness--that we can come to Him the first, second, and tenth time we are guilty of a particular sin, but we dare not come to Him with the 20th (or 50th) infraction against a specific commandment. This erroneous thinking causes many sincere Christians to throw up their hands in despair and to avoid doing the very thing that would help them--running to their heavenly Father for forgiveness and help.

Point your students back to the grace of God. We are justified by grace. And we are sanctified in the same way--freely by God's grace. We cannot, with our own power, "clean up our act." The Holy Spirit working in our hearts and lives through His Word enables the necessary changes in behavior. He changes us as we allow Him to do so. With His power we can avoid that sin in the future.

Someone who says, "I'll come to Jesus when I'm ready to give up drinking (smoking, beating my wife, etc.)," betrays a misunderstanding of God's grace. But so does a Christian who says, "I'll confess this sin to God after I've avoided it for three days (weeks, months, etc.)."

As Paul wrote, "**It is God who works in you to will and to act according to His good purpose**" (Phil. 2:13). Help students reassure one another of these facts.

CAN I BE SURE? (Objectives 3 and 4)

Use this section to tie together the two main thoughts of Jesus' discourse in **John 14:1-14**. Both here and in **1 John 5:14-15** Scripture connects the assurance of forgiveness and eternal life with confident, powerful prayer. Help students see that unless we know the truth that our sins are forgiven for Jesus' sake, we cannot approach God confidently to ask Him for the things we need for ourselves or to intercede for the needs of others. But knowing Jesus as the way to the Father, knowing the truth of our forgiveness and God's love for us, and having the gift of eternal life, we can come to God in prayer as Luther describes it, "As dear children ask their dear Father."

Reading assignment for next time: **John 14:15-31 and 16:5-16**

Session 32: The Promise of the Spirit

BIBLE BASIS: John 14:15-31; 16:5-16

CENTRAL TRUTH

Before He went to the cross, Jesus promised to send the Holy Spirit to live in His disciples in a new and powerful way. The Spirit would teach, comfort, encourage, counsel, and help all believers who lived after Pentecost.

OBJECTIVES

That the students will:
1. Explain the sanctifying role of the Holy Spirit as He testifies to us about Jesus
2. Find comfort in the Holy Spirit's work on their behalf
3. Rely on the Spirit's counsel, especially during times of crisis, difficulty, or decision-making

BACKGROUND

The Holy Spirit ministers to New Testament believers in ways most of us probably never think too much about. Yet what a blessing the Spirit is to us! In today's assigned Scripture readings, Jesus spells out some of the details of the Holy Spirit's ministry.

The Greek word translated "Counselor" in the NIV has sometimes been transliterated as "Paraclete." We have no really precise English equivalent for this name/title. It can be rendered literally, "one called along side another to help." Thus, some translators have chosen to use the title, "Helper."

Others have chosen "Advocate" instead. The word originally meant, at least by implication, one who spoke in court on behalf of another. Jesus Himself is called our Paraclete in **1 John 2:1**. ("If any man sin, we have an Advocate [Paraclete] with the Father" -- KJV) The English word counselor often carries this connotation today--we refer to lawyers as "legal counsel," for example. Attorneys, especially those for the defense, are often addressed as "counselor."

Whatever word we choose, the meaning of the name Paraclete given the Holy Spirit by Jesus can be derived from what the Savior says in describing the Spirit's ministry on behalf of believers. His description is sprinkled throughout **John 14--16**. Skim these chapters before you continue preparing this lesson. List the facts you find about the Holy Spirit, His character, His attributes, His relationship to the Father and the Son, and His ministry on the behalf of believers. Behind each item, jot down what that fact means when applied to your own life.

Then pray for yourself and for your students. Ask the Spirit to help you communicate these truths and their application in a clear and meaningful way to each of the young people in your class.

GETTING INTO THE LESSON (Objectives 1 and 2)

Have a volunteer read through the four paragraphs that introduce this lesson in the Student Book. Briefly acknowledge the difficulty we sometimes have in understanding the ministry of the Holy Spirit. Good experiences with an earthly father can help us relate to the concept of God as our heavenly Father. Jesus became a human being for us. The Scriptures refer to Him as our Brother. We have very little difficulty understanding that kind of relationship. But when we come to the activity of the Holy Spirit, we often experience more difficulty in understanding precisely who this Person of the Trinity is and what what He does on our behalf.

OUR TEACHER (Objectives 1 and 2)

Before looking at what Jesus says about the Holy Spirit in today's Bible reading, have the students describe their concept of a perfect teacher as directed in the Student Book. Let them complete this activity on their own, and then share thoughts and ideas with one another.

Then ask them to skim **John 14--16** to find clues about what the Holy Spirit does as our teacher. You may wish to have the students each work with a partner as they look for this information. The directions in the Student Book ask them to outline the information on the lines provided, keeping in mind that they will later write a complete paragraph in their notebook.

After everyone has finished, share comments and insights with one another. You will probably wish to include these ideas:

The Holy Spirit, as our Teacher, knows God's truth thoroughly. He has the ability to explain that truth to us perfectly, not just so that we understand it with our mind, but also with our heart. The Spirit is the "Spirit of Truth," who teaches us the truth--the truth that sets us free **(John 8:32)**. The text also makes it clear that the Holy Spirit always points us to Jesus. You may also wish to emphasize that, as our Teacher, the Holy Spirit helps us remember what He has taught us. He brings God's truth to our minds when we need it in a given situation. Remind the students that they can ask the Holy Spirit to do this for specific situations in which they need God's help to live and walk in love and obedience.

OUR COUNSELOR (Objectives 1, 2, and 3)

If necessary, develop the concept of what a human counselor does for his or her clients. Ask in what situations people sometimes consult with counselors. You may mention individuals who are looking for a job for the first time, or who are dissatisfied with their present job and are looking for a new one; people who are experiencing difficulty with their marriage; parents who have problems with their children; etc. After this brief discussion, ask students to jot their answer to the questions in the Student Book about what the perfect counselor would be like. Again, let students work through this task on their own and then compare notes with the entire class.

If students were working with a partner previously, ask them to work with that same person again while they skim **John 14--16** one more time. Remind them that they will use the information they find as the basis for a paragraph in their notebooks later on in the period.

Share answers with one another after everyone has finished gathering information. Point out that the word translated <u>counselor</u> in this part of Scripture, is really the Greek word <u>Paraclete</u>. Share information from the **"Background"** section of this guide that you feel appropriate for your group. You may want to have your students jot notes to themselves about this important New Testament word.

As you talk about the Holy Spirit as our Counselor, you will want to bring out these points: The Holy Spirit is one Counselor whose "office is always open"--He's always with us because Jesus promised that the Holy Spirit lives in believers. The Holy Spirit as our Counselor completely understands us and our feelings, even when we don't understand ourselves. He loves us with perfect love. He always tells us what we need to hear. He convicts us of our sin and comforts us with the Good News of God's forgiveness for us in Christ. He helps us know what to do and He gives us the power to do it. He understands our weakness and He share God's strength with us. He brings God's peace to our hearts despite the turmoil of outward situations and circumstances. What a comfort He is!

Ask students to share situations in which they would appreciate having a perfect counselor to help them with their problems. Ask for volunteers to share specific times that the Holy Spirit has ministered to them in this way in their lives. Share one or two instances from your own life as well.

OUR INTERCESSOR (Objectives 2 and 3)

Have **Rom. 8:26-28** read aloud from as many different Bible versions as possible. Then ask individual students to paraphrase these verses in their own words.

Use more than one English dictionary to find the meaning of the words intercede and intercessor. Be sure also to consult a Bible dictionary. Have the students record the various meanings of these two words as the definitions are read.

Discuss the two questions from the Student Book. At some time during the discussion, share the idea that the Holy Spirit prays for us according to God's perfect will. He continually carries on this ministry of intercession, even when we do not or cannot pray for ourselves.

Because Holy Spirit intercedes for us in accordance with God's will, we can know for sure that in all things God works for our good as **Rom. 8:28** promises us.

GOD'S SPIRIT--MY HELPER

This section outlines for your students the four-paragraph paper they are asked to write, summarizing the findings they have made during today's study. Explain the instructions as necessary, especially transitions between paragraphs, and then allow students to begin work in class. Ask that they finish their paper as homework.

Reading assignment for next time: John 15:1-17

Note: You may wish to assign all or parts of the Bible study in session 33 for students to complete before the next class period. See the material in this guide for that session.

Session 33: Abiding in Christ

BIBLE BASIS: John 15:1-17

CENTRAL TRUTH

Faith in Jesus as our Savior connects us in a living relationship with God. When we abide in Jesus, we will demonstrate our faith as we practice love and obedience to Christ. God the Holy Spirit continually empowers us to produce the kind of fruit that causes us to become more and more like Jesus.

OBJECTIVES

That the students will:

1. Describe spiritual fruit and how God's grace enables believers bear it
2. Evaluate the "fruit of the Spirit" evident in their own lives
3. "Abide in the vine" as they study God's Word and use the Sacraments and thus be enabled to bear more and more of the fruit of the Spirit
4. Use Bible dictionaries and concordances to study one fruit of the Spirit in depth

BACKGROUND

In just 7 verses, Jesus repeats and highlights several important themes about which He has taught throughout His ministry. He once again explains His relationship with His Father. He uses the metaphor of a vine and its branches to emphasize the crucial importance of having a living, personal relationship with Himself. He points out that such a faith relationship will result in a life of love. We bear fruit, much fruit, as a natural outcome of this living relationship and thus bring glory to our heavenly Father.

Just as an orange tree doesn't have to try and try and try to bear oranges, neither can we depend on our own efforts to produce love, joy, peace, patience, kindness, gentleness, goodness, faithfulness, or self-control. An orange tree bears oranges because it's an orange tree. Christ's people bear fruit because they abide in Him by His grace. We love because of who we are as His brothers and sisters. We love, because by His unimaginable grace He loved us first.

The temptation to use God's law to "motivate" our students is often very strong for those of us who deal with teens day after day. Telling students what they should, ought, and must do often seems so much easier and more effective than trusting the Gospel to do its work. We know, though, that the Law has no ability to empower us. By the Law comes the knowledge of sin, and our students, like all believers, do need to realize their sin.

But only by grace can the young people in our classrooms become the men and women of God He has planned for them to be. They can bear fruit only as God's Spirit produces that fruit in their hearts.

Before you continue with today's preparation, pray that the Spirit will open your students' eyes to see their "fruit-bearing potential." Pray that you can help them clearly divide Law and Gospel as they study this text together.

GETTING INTO THE LESSON (Objective 3)

Work through the introductory material in the Student Book with the class. Talk together briefly about the questions in the last paragraph. Your aim should be to establish the fact that we learn to know people as we spend time with them. Usually the more time we spend listening to one another and doing things together, the better we come to know the other person.

ABIDING IN JESUS (Objectives 1 and 3)

Read **John 15:1-17** together and ask a few questions to make sure that your students have understood what Jesus says in these verses. To evaluate their understanding, have them summarize the verses themselves on the lines provided in the Student Book. Check with the students as they work to determine the kinds of comments that they are making. Correct any misimpressions that surface. The text is fairly self-explanatory. You may wish to highlight the process of pruning and how it helps the growth process; the idea of abiding in Jesus or remaining in Him; the truth that as we bear fruit we bring glory to God; and the agape love that Jesus showed as He laid down His life for us, His friends.

BEARING MUCH FRUIT (Objectives 1, 2, and 4)

It may be best to assign this section of the lesson as homework the day before you intend to discuss it in class. Session 32 suggested this option.

If students have not yet completed this section on their own, have them work independently during the class period today. Give individuals help as necessary. Students will need concordances, dictionaries, Bible dictionaries, and Biblical topical wordbooks to complete the exercises. If they did the section as homework, share information and insights, questions and concerns with each other.

As the class gets to the Analyze section toward the end of the activity, explore the questions asked there together. Use the explanations given in the "Background" section of this guide as information to share with the class. Be sure to use a Law/Gospel approach. Acknowledge the fact that just as we are justified by God's grace, so we are also sanctified by His grace. God forgives us when we fail to produce the fruit of the Spirit in our lives. His Spirit also works in our hearts to empower us to become more and more fruitful in His service.

At this point, go back to the text from **John 15**. Discuss specifically the term <u>abiding in Jesus.</u> Talk about what that means in a practical sense. You will want to refer students back to the introductory section of this lesson, in which they thought about spending time with a special person in order to get to know that person better. "Abiding in Jesus" involves spending time with Him--in His Word-- and, too, making use of the Sacraments as His means of grace. Discuss the term <u>means of grace</u> with the class from the viewpoint that these are the means (or instruments or channels) through which God offers and gives the grace of His forgiveness.

The two "tell about" questions at the end of this section in the Student Book asks students to share specific instances in their life when a particular fruit of the Spirit was present or absent. Ask for volunteers to share this kind of information. Encourage students to become as specific and "real" as possible. For example, many Christians experience challenges to their self-control brought about by a quick temper. Talk about anger at parents, teachers, younger brothers or sisters, and so on, from the perspective of the fruit of the Spirit--patience, self-control, joy, or love.

At this point in the class discussion, ask the students to open their notebook and write the letter to Jesus assigned in the Student Book. This should serve as a confession/ absolution activity with which to end the class period. Make plans to collect and read the notebooks at an early date.

<u>Reading assignment for next time:</u>
John 15:18-27

Session 34: Standing Against the World

BIBLE BASIS: John 15:18-27

CENTRAL TRUTH

The world system in which we find ourselves actively opposes God's plan and God's people. Yet, we can live victoriously despite this opposition as we rely on the power of the Holy Spirit, our Counselor.

OBJECTIVES

That the students will:
1. Explain what Scripture means when it uses the term <u>world</u>
2. Describe the conflict between the temptations and demands of the world system and the claims of Christ
3. Trust God's power to enable them to withstand the pressures of the world system as they go on working and witnessing for Jesus

BACKGROUND

"You can't beat the system!" How often we have heard this--maybe even said it ourselves.

While He still lived on earth, Jesus warned His followers that the "system" would oppose them. It would oppose their witness and attempt to smother their faith. 1 John 5:19: **"We know that we are children of God, and that the whole world is under the control of the evil one."** The world system in which we find ourselves does not applaud us for clinging to the Christian hope. We can expect persecution, and we do well to prepare for it.

If that were the sum total of what you will convey to your class today, what a grim picture it would make! But the Lord Jesus did not stop after He pronounced His warning. Instead, He repeated His promise to send the Counselor--the Holy Spirit--to strengthen His followers.

The Spirit of truth would testify about Jesus. The Spirit would keep on reminding God's people of the truth even as the world bombarded them with lie after lie. The Spirit would encourage and empower Jesus' followers to go on testifying to the truth they knew, the truth He Himself had taught them. We are not alone. The Holy Spirit ministers to each of us today, in all the ways Jesus promised.

The students in your class know that living as Christ's people is not easy in a world that actively seeks to dissuade them. They face subtle peer pressure at times, and perhaps outright ridicule at other times. Those who trust Jesus and live in love, selflessness, and obedience can expect rejection by many who still live "in the world."

The Good News you will share with your class today is that we can beat the system. Jesus has given us victory over the world's way of thinking and over the world's way of doing things. He promised, **John 16:33: "I have told you these things, so that in Me you may have peace. In this world you will have trouble. But take heart! I have overcome the world."**

GETTING INTO THE LESSON (Objective 2)

To introduce today's topic, discuss the stories with which the Student Book material begins. After you have gone through all four of these, ask which situation would be the most difficult to face. If possible, get the students to identify possible reasons for this difficulty.

THE PRESENT WORLD SYSTEM
(Objective 1)

Read through today's text together. Ask someone to define the word persecute. Then point out the degree of animosity the world will feel toward us. Ask what the "world" did to Jesus.

Let the students write their own definition of the "world" in their Student Books on the appropriate lines before you go on. Their definitions will probably be quite fuzzy. Then continue by reading together the texts listed. At that point, ask students to work individually to rewrite their definition. Share these with one another.

You will want to make sure that they identify the "world" as the entire present world system. It includes a consistent way of thinking or life-view. As the term is used in the passages you read, it refers to an orientation to living, a view of reality. This view is continually hostile to God, to God's plan, and to God's people.

"THE WORLD" IN MY WORLD (Objectives 2 and 3)

Work through the material in this section quickly. By now, most of the information listed here should be fairly self-evident to your students.

If the class has trouble identifying places in which their Christian values system conflicts with that of the world, ask them to think about the introductory stories in this lesson; advertisements on television, radio, and in magazines; their friends' values; etc. Attempt to pin students down to identifying these conflicts in their own personal lives. What represents a real conflict for each of them individually?

To close this section, ask about times when we give in to the pressure from the world's system in which we live.

VICTORY OVER THE WORLD (Objective 3)

Assure the students that our Lord Jesus knows how strong the conflicts we face really are. He knows that we cannot stand alone. That's why He promised us His Holy Spirit.

Discuss your need for God's power in your life. Reassure one another with God's forgiveness. Encourage one another, using the promise of the Holy Spirit's power. This power will help us to keep on standing firm in faith. It will give us the desire and the ability to keep on testifying to Jesus, no matter what conflicts we confront in the world.

Reading assignment for next time: **John 17**

Session 35: Jesus Prays for His People (Part 1)

BIBLE BASIS: John 17

CENTRAL TRUTH

As our great High Priest, our Lord Jesus continually intercedes before the Father's throne on our behalf. That thought comforts us and also encourages us in our ministry of intercession for others, especially for our brothers and sisters in the body of Christ.

OBJECTIVES

That the students will:
1. Explain what Jesus' high-priestly role involves
2. Analyze Jesus' high-priestly prayer from **John 17** and select specific petitions to pray for themselves and for others
3. Practice praying aloud with one or two other Christians
4. Describe the need for unity of faith when praying with others
5. Want to pray, both alone and together with other believers more often

BACKGROUND

During this session and the next, you and your students will work through Jesus' high-priestly prayer and its meaning for us as His followers today. On first reading, ninth-graders may find much that seems abstract and foreign to their way of thinking. Yet as they study the prayer, the depth of Jesus' concern for them should become more and more apparent. While no Christian fully understands all the implications of Jesus' role as our Intercessor, sessions 35 and 36 should help students begin to see the rich comfort this concept can give us.

Even when I don't know what to pray for myself, even when I don't **want** to pray for myself, Jesus stands at the right hand of the Father praying for me. And because His prayers always agree fully with the Father's perfect will for me, I can rest confidently in the knowledge that His prayers for me will be answered by my gracious heavenly Father. What a blessing!

Knowing that the Savior intercedes for me widens my vision of my own role as intercessor. As Peter wrote, **"You are a chosen people, a royal priesthood" (1 Peter 2:9).** We believe in the priesthood of all believers. That truth confers on us the great privilege and the great responsibility of intercessory prayer.

How different the church would be if each believer were to take the role of intercessor more seriously! How different our world would be if the prayers of Christ's church were more consistent and more fervent!

Look over the material from both session 35 and session 36. Decide which activities you would like the students to complete in class, which you will assign as homework, and which might best be designated as optional extra-credit assignments. Think about the special needs of the students in each class you teach as you make your decision.

GETTING INTO THE LESSON (Objective 5)

To stimulate your students to begin thinking about their own personal prayer life, have them complete the inventory on the first page of this lesson in their Student Books on their own. Assure them that no one will look at their responses unless they choose to share those answers. You will return to this inventory again as you work through session 36. For now, simply let them complete the inventory and move on to the next section of the Student Book.

HOW AND WHAT JESUS PRAYED
(Objectives 1 and 2)

Work through the questions in this section together in class. The answers to the first fill-in-the-blanks activity are:
They <u>offered sacrifices</u>.
They <u>prayed for</u> the <u>people</u>.
They <u>taught</u> the <u>people</u>.
Compare Jesus' ministry of teaching and intercession with that of the Old Testament priesthood. **Heb. 7:27**

explains the difference between Jesus' sacrifice and the ones made by the Old Testament priests.

Help students list the various petitions Jesus prayed. The list your class develops may vary somewhat from the answers given below. These are intended as a guideline for your use as you walk your students through Jesus' prayer.

For Himself (vv. 1-5)
1. Glorify Me as Your Son.
2. Glorify Me in Your presence.

For His Disciples Then (vv. 6-19)
1. Keep them safe by the power of Your name.
2. Give them fulness of joy in their hearts.
3. Keep them from the Evil One.
4. Sanctify them through Your truth.

For Us and All Believers (vv. 20-26)
1. Give them unity/make them one.
2. Help them live in Me as I live in them.
3. Let the world know that the Father sent and loves the Son.
4. Let them live with Me in My glory.
5. Let Your love show in their lives.

As an alternative to working through the activity together in class, let students work in small groups to complete the chart and then compare their answers with those of others in the class. Answer the questions that follow the chart, especially the questions students have about what Jesus meant by individual petitions He prayed. Also lead the students to apply each petition to themselves personally. Note that though originally Jesus prayed (**vv. 6-19**) for His disciples at that time, we can be sure He prays for us too.

FOR ME! (Objectives 2, 3, and 5)
Have individuals complete and then share the answers that they write in this section. This part of the class period is designed to provide an opportunity for the young people to share their faith with one another and to assure one another of Jesus' forgiveness for times they have been less than faithful in their own prayer lives. Read **John 17:20-26** to the students, asking them to listen as though Jesus Himself were praying that prayer for them. Use the translation or paraphrase you feel would most clearly express for your students what is on Jesus' heart as He intercedes for us.

Close today's class period with prayer for one another. Model your prayers on Jesus' prayer. If your students feel comfortable praying aloud, by all means encourage them to do so. Or they may pray silently for one another. Remind them to pray for you and encourage them to continue their prayers for you and for one another until you meet in your next class session.

Reading assignment for next time: **John 17**

Session 36: Jesus Prays for His People (Part 2)

BIBLE BASIS: John 17

CENTRAL TRUTH
See session 35.

OBJECTIVES
See session 35.

BACKGROUND
See session 35.

GETTING INTO THE LESSON (Objectives 1 and 2)
Briefly review the concepts from session 35, especially Jesus' high-priestly role as our Intercessor. Then have someone read **1 Peter 2:9** and **1 Tim. 2:1**. Ask if the students have ever thought of themselves in the role of "priest" or "intercessor." If we truly are a "royal priesthood," what does that imply? What duties and privileges are ours?

MODELS OF INTERCESSION (Objectives 4 and 5)

Have students read the references listed in the chart and complete it by supplying the missing information. Then ask what things we may include (should include) as we intercede for others. The implication from the model intercessory prayers we see in Scripture is that we may ask for others anything we ask for ourselves—stronger faith, forgiveness, the power of the Holy Spirit, physical healing, success in our lives, more love, increasing knowledge, more spiritual fruit, and so on.

As time permits, look at Paul's intercessory prayers for the Corinthians **(2 Cor. 13:9)** and **(Colossians 1:9-14)**. Let students us topical wordbooks or concordances to find other instances of intercession in Scripture.

LEARNING TO PRAY (Objectives 4 and 5)

Direct the students to look back at the prayer inventory they completed at the beginning of session 35. Ask them to review their responses and to comment on them if they would like. Do they see any places in which they wish they could improve?

Read the Student Book material from the section together in class. This material is meant to reassure them. None of us need feel awkward at not knowing how to pray as fluently as we wish we did. All of us need to learn many things about prayer. So did Peter, John, and Jesus' other disciples. We learn by doing.

The three passages from **Matt.**, **Acts**, and **Rom.** emphasize Jesus' presence to hear and to do for us what we ask, God's power and willingness to answer us, and the need to be specific when we pray. Draw these three main points out during a brief class discussion.

If students have difficulty filling in the three blanks at the end of this section of their lesson ("**Jesus prayed for . . .**"), refer them to the chart from session 35.

MAKING A LIST (Objectives 3 and 5)

The directions for this activity have been printed in the Student Book. Explain them as necessary. It would probably be best to let each student choose his/her own partner. Joint prayer is a rather personal, intimate activity. Students need to feel comfortable with their prayer partner.

Supply three, four, or five cards or slips of paper to each student. As they jot notes on these cards, encourage them to include their parents, pastors, teachers, foreign missionaries, people "in the news," and others on their cards. As they note those things for which they will pray, encourage them to be specific.

Keep in mind that one activity during one class period will not give students the practice that they need to become as comfortable and as effective as possible in their prayers. Therefore, you may wish to repeat this activity in the days and weeks ahead. At some time in the future, the cards will probably no longer be necessary. If you intend to make this a long-term class activity, encourage students to write their prayer requests and the dates of these prayers in their class notebook. That way they can keep track of God's answers and praise Him for them!

Note: Session 37 is a review/evaluation activity. Remind students to look over the list of key words from the previous units and to reread especially the texts you have covered during the time since your last evaluation.

Reading assingment for next time: Review **John 11--17**.

Session 37: Concluding Activities for Unit 3

BIBLE BASIS: John 11--17

See the note regarding evaluation in session 11. Some possible test items have been printed below for your convenience. Feel free to alter them to fit your particular instruction situation.

SUGGESTED MULTIPLE CHOICE QUESTIONS

1. Caiaphas was (a) a disciple of Jesus (b) a Roman official (c) a man whose feet Jesus washed (d) the High Priest **(d)**
2. To anoint someone meant that you (a) poured oil or perfume on them (b) forgave them (c) condemned them (d) washed their hands **(a)**
3. The disciple who betrayed Jesus was (a) Philip (b) Simon (c) Judas (d) Thomas **(c)**
4. The Jewish feast celebrated by Jesus on the night He was betrayed was (a) the Feast of Tabernacles (b) the Feast of Dedication (c) the Festival of Pentecost (d) Passover **(d)**
5. The Holy Spirit is given all these names in Scripture except (a) Counselor (b) Savior (c) Helper (d) Teacher **(b)**
6. Jesus' "hour of glory" was really His (a) anointing (b) death (c) resurrection (d) trial **(b)**
7. The Greek word for love among friends is (a) agape (b) eros (c) phileo **(c)**
8. The Greek word for romantic love, the emotion of love is (a) eros (b) agape (c) phileo **(a)**
9. Lazarus was the man (a) Jesus raised from the dead (b) who carried Jesus' cross (c) who washed Jesus' feet (d) who told Peter about Jesus **(a)**
10. To witness your faith means to (a) deny it (b) share it (c) pray for growth (d) question if it is true or not **(b)**
11. Cosmos refers to (a) a new video game (b) a candy bar (c) the world system that opposes God and God's plan (d) a permanent space station lanuched by France. **(c)**

SUGGESTED SHORT ANSWER QUESTIONS

1. When Jesus washed the disciples' feet, what was He teaching His followers?
2. Why is Jesus' death referred to as a victory? What or who was the enemy? What was won or defeated?
3. Jesus calls the Holy Spirit the believer's Counselor. Explain how the Holy Spirit is a Counselor in your life.
4. Suppose an unbelieving friend would ask you, "What do you mean when you say you have faith in Jesus?" How would you respond?
5. Why is it important to you that Jesus is "the true Vine"?
6. Many people often feel afraid to love other people. They hold back their love for various reasons. Perhaps you have felt that way about a family member, a friend, or a teacher. What reasons can you identify for a person's fear and reluctance to love others?
7. In what three ways has and does Jesus serve as your High Priest?
8. Jesus proclaims Himself to be the Way, the Truth, and the Life. Why is that such great news for you as a believer?
9. What motivates believers to give to God and God's kingdom? Explain your answer in 20 words or less.
10. What was Jesus' top priority when He lived on earth? List three specific ways He accomplished this.
11. How does simply regretting sin differ from repentance?
12. Explain agape love.
13. Choose one fruit of the Spirit. Explain what it is and how it shows up in the life of believers. Give two specific examples from your own life or from the life of someone you know.

Feel free to duplicate the above questions for use in testing. Please add the following credit line: Concordia Publishing House, copyright 1986. **Used by permission.**

Unit 4: Crucified and Risen

As the unit title suggests, this unit covers the passion and resurrection accounts from John's gospel. In dealing with this material, it is especially critical that you go beyond the historical facts to the heart of the message--and from there to the hearts of your students.

What does it say?
What does it mean?
What does it mean to me?

Pray for special grace from the Holy Spirit to be able to convey the depth of what Jesus' death and rising again mean for the everyday life of each individual in your classroom.

PLANNING THE UNIT

Session 38: The session suggests various methods you may use to give your class an overview of the passion account and its meaning for their lives. The methods suggested include films, books, slides, and musical recordings. You will need to order or gather these items in advance.

Session 43: Order materials from the Board for Professional Education Services to encourage students to consider full-time professional ministry in the church. See the introduction to the session in this guide for the address and further details.

Session 38: Jesus Died for Me! (Part 1)

BIBLE BASIS: John 18--21

CENTRAL TRUTH

God loved the world so much that He sent His one and only Son to die and rise again for us. Whoever believes in Him will not die eternally, but will receive forgiveness of sins and everlasting life as a gift of God's grace.

OBJECTIVES

That the students will:
1. Summarize the flow of events from Jesus' passion
2. Explain that their sins nailed Jesus to the cross, but that His love for them held Him there
3. Describe the Father's love for them in Christ in a fuller and richer way than before
4. Share with one another their reactions to God's love and thus encourage one another in their faith

BACKGROUND

In perfect love He dies,
For me; He dies for me!
O, all-atoning Sacrifice
I cling by faith to Thee!

The Lutheran Hymnal, 170, stanza 5

Not one of us can comprehend fully what happened on the hill of Golgatha that dark Friday nearly 2,000 years ago. Perhaps the most incomprehensible part for us is our own personal involvement. Our sins caused His death. Our sins nailed Jesus to the cross. But the nails did not hold Him there--His love did! His love for us and His Father's love for us are that big. What a merciful God we serve!

This is the first of two lessons dealing with Jesus' passion. The two have been designed to give students an overview of the last four chapters of John's gospel, which share the account of Jesus' death and resurrection. After students have looked at the sweep of the events and the meaning of those events for their own lives, they will go back to examine the various details John includes in **chapters 18--21**.

Consider the various options suggested in this lesson plan and the plan for session 39. Then choose those activities that will best help your particular students grasp the most important truth they will ever hear: Jesus died for each of us and rose again that we could have eternal life by faith in Him.

GETTING INTO THE LESSON (Objectives 1, 2, and 3)

This lesson will consist of input for student thought and consideration. Students will then be asked to write a reaction paper, poem, or essay. Or they may complete one of the projects suggested below. They will share their work sometime during the rest of the course. You may want to schedule the sharing for your next class period. Or you may want to give students more time to work on their response, especially if they are writing longer pieces or doing art projects.

Here are some options for you to consider as today's in-class activity:

1. Show a film based on the meaning of Jesus' suffering, death, and resurrection. Among those you may find appropriate are The Ant Keeper, Sacrifice, and Greater Love. All three of these are parablelike, but readily interpreted by young teens. All are available for rental through Concordia Publishing House. Check their film rental catalog for other appropriate films.

2. Artists and musicians throughout history have responded to the Savior's passion and resurrection in various ways. Many art museums in major cities loan color slides of major art works. Lenten and Easter hymns carry with them a tremendous potential for touching our emotions and making the meaning of Jesus' death and resurrection both real and personal. Show appropriate slides or play recordings to share some of this music and art with your students. Don't overlook contemporary Christian musicians. Several Christian artists such as Don Francisco and The Second Chapter of Acts have produced music that may be appropriate and meaningful to your class.

As an alternative to writing a reaction paper, you may want to help your students to put together a presentation, including both art and music, that could be shown in a school chapel service.

3. Have someone tape a dramatic reading of the Passion history, perhaps from a harmony of the gospel accounts. Think about putting music in the background at appropriate places. Play it for the students. Incorporate **Ps. 22** and **Is. 53** into the reading.

4. Read selected portions of the book by Jim Bishop, The Day Christ Died. While Bishop was not a Christian when he wrote this book (and freely admits that fact in the book's preface), he captures much of the gross injustice and much of the terrible agony the Savior endured. Jesus' enemies and His disciples come alive as Bishop analyzes their motives. Bishop researched customs of the time quite thoroughly and presents an intriguing portrait of what went on during the last week of Jesus' earthly life.

You may wish to suggest that interested students read the entire book and report to the class as an extra credit assignment.

5. Use the two stories included in the Student Book for session 38. Read each to the class while they sit with their eyes closed imagining the feelings of the characters involved.

(**Note:** The second story, "Sacrifice," is based on a true incident that happened in St. Louis, MO, on April 9, 1985.)

After you have read the stories, discuss the questions printed in the Student Book. Then ask students to respond in writing. Their book suggests a letter to a friend telling about what their Friend Jesus did for them. You may wish to offer alternatives such as a poem, song or hymn, an essay, or even an art project. Check with art or English teachers in your school for suggestions and other alternatives. You may be able to make an assignment jointly.

Reading assignment for next time:
John 18--21

Session 39: Jesus Died for Me! (Part 2)

BIBLE BASIS: John 18--21

CENTRAL TRUTH
See session 38.

OBJECTIVES
See session 38.

BACKGROUND
See session 38.

GETTING INTO THE LESSON (Objectives 1, 2, 3, and 4)

Your plans for today's class session will depend heavily on the choices you made as you selected activities for session 38. You will probably want to use most of today's class period sharing the papers and/or projects the students produced in response to the film, movie, book, or stories you shared during session 38.

If you have time at the end of the period, use the chancel drama found in the Student Book material for session 39. Consider the possibility of presenting this drama for your whole school during a chapel service.

Whether or not you intend to do this, discuss the drama as time permits. The Student Book contains three brief discussion questions. Use them to tie the Bible reading from **John 18--21** together with the drama. Because Jesus did suffer, die, and rise again, God can show mercy to us. He can forgive us of our sins. He offers us eternal life with Him by His grace. Personalize the Gospel as you discuss the drama.

Reading assignment for next time: **John 18:1-11**

Session 40: The Cup of God's Wrath

BIBLE BASIS: John 18:1-11

CENTRAL TRUTH

Jesus received the complete punishment that we deserved because of our sin. All God's wrath rested on Him. Because Jesus took all our sin upon Himself, God credits each believer with all of Jesus' righteousness.

OBJECTIVES

That the students will:
1. Explain the Biblical imagery of the "cup of God's wrath"
2. Describe the seriousness of sin and how it separates the sinner from God
3. Thank Jesus that He has done all that was necessary for their salvation and that He drank the "cup of God's wrath" for us

BACKGROUND

He was oppressed and afflicted,
Yet He did not open His mouth;
He was led like a lamb to the slaughter,
And as a sheep before her shearers is silent,
So He did not open His mouth . . .
He was cut off from the land of the living;
For the transgression of My people He was stricken . . . .
It was the Lord's will
To crush Him and cause Him to suffer,
And though the Lord makes His life a guilt offering,
He will see His offspring and prolong His days,
And the will of the Lord
Will prosper in His hand.
                    Is. 53: 7-10

What an incredibly detailed picture the prophet Isaiah painted of the vicarious atonement! Seven centuries before the Messiah was born Isaiah described Jesus' agony in exquisite detail. More incredible than the timing, the meaning of the prophecy overwhelms us.

Who could have believed God would love sinners so very much? Who could have thought the Father would be willing to give the life of His only begotten Son for our redemption? Who could have imagined that the Son would be willing to pay such a tremendous price? The Father gave His Son. The Son gave His life.

Jesus drank the cup of God's wrath to the last drop. Now, we drink the cup of blessing instead. Today's session material focuses on the contrast between the cup of God's wrath and the cup of God's blessing. Before you continue your lesson preparation, pray that your students will be led by the Holy Spirit to recognize more clearly their sin and their need for a Redeemer. Pray too, that they will clearly see the complete redemption that is theirs by faith in the Son of God.

GETTING INTO THE LESSON

Ask students to open their Bibles to **John 18**. Remind them that the incident recorded here took place in the Garden of Gethsemane on Maundy Thursday evening after the Passover meal. Ask them to use a piece of paper to jot down what they think Jesus meant by His question in **verse 11**. Note that the Student Book suggests they read **Matt. 26:39** before they answer.

After they have finished, ask volunteers to share what they have written. Listen carefully to the ideas the students have, but don't comment at this time as to whether their explanations are right or wrong. Simply tell the class you will return to this activity later.

Ask students to identify the most bitter medicine they have ever tasted. Do they remember their feelings as they anticipated having to take each dose?

THE CUP OF GOD'S WRATH

The passage from Jeremiah is part of a larger section from this prophet declaring in a very powerful way the imminent judgment of God. Read the verses together after you explain briefly Jeremiah's prophetic role. Remind students that God's feelings toward sin do not change over time. The anger He describes here remains the same today.

Then have students read the poem printed in their books. It rephrases the prophecy from Jeremiah to express feelings the prophet surely must have had as God's judgment was revealed to him by the Holy Spirit.

Discuss any parts of the poem for which students need help in understanding. Then have them independently answer the question printed at the end of the poem. Share responses when everyone has finished.

The Old Testament references listed here are not an exhaustive list of Biblical passages that allude to the "cup of wrath." You may want to have your students compare two vivid New Testament passages--**Rev. 14:9-10** and **16:19-21**.

Is. 51:21-22 has a strong Gospel accent. We will never drink the cup of God's wrath again--He promises! He promises us mercy instead of judgment.

THE CUP OF SALVATION

After students have had a chance to guess about the fill-ins on this page, have everyone complete the sentences:

Jesus drank the cup of God's wrath.

Now God offers us the cup of salvation.

Discuss the meaning of **Ps. 116:12-19**. The psalmist was not writing about Holy Communion. However, as we commune we remember and share Jesus' blood--the very blood by which our salvation was secured. Our hearts overflow with gratitude to God for His grace.

The last paragraphs of this lesson call for a response by the students. Before they begin writing, personalize God's wrath and His mercy by asking them to place themselves in Jeremiah's vision. Suppose we were handed God's chalice of wrath and were told to drink? Why would God be justified in demanding that? Now suppose Jesus stepped beside us and took the chalice out of our hands. Suppose He drank it instead. Suppose the Father allowed His Son to do this to make us all His sons and daughters. How would that make you feel? What would you say to God? Write it!

<u>Reading Assignment for next time</u>: **John 18:12--19:16**

Session 41: On Trial

BIBLE BASIS: John 18:12--19:16

CENTRAL TRUTH

Jesus willingly submitted Himself to the death sentence. The charges against Him were false. The demands that He be crucified, unjust. He became obedient unto death, even death on a cross, because He loved us.

OBJECTIVES

That the students will:
1. Analyze Jesus' trials and debate the justness of these trials
2. Explain Jesus' claim that His kingdom is not of this world and His claim that everyone on the side of truth listens to Him
3. Identify the hatred in their own lives and repent of it
4. Receive the assurance that God for Jesus' sake forgives all their sins, even the sins of injustice and hatred

BACKGROUND

This lesson traces the events that transpired between Jesus' arrest in the Garden of Gethsemane up to and including the moment in which Pontius Pilate pronounced the sentence of death on the Savior. The scribes and chief priests pressed Pilate for crucifixion. Although they had first tried Him on the charge of blasphemy, they accused Jesus of treason when He was arraigned before Pilate. They implied that Jesus was a dangerous political rebel. While Pilate almost certainly did not believe this charge, his own political future was in jeopardy. Therefore, under pressure, he yielded to the will of the crowd.

As we read this section of Scripture, images flash back and forth across the screens of our mind:

We see the unfairness, the injustice, of everything that happened. We cringe to think that the disciples all left the Savior, afraid for their own lives.

We see Peter deny again and again even knowing Jesus. And we recall the tears of remorse he cried later.

We see God working in history to fulfill His prophetic Word. All the prophets had pointed to a death like that which Jesus suffered. We see Jews and Gentiles alike participating in the execution of God's one and only Son.

We see Pilate asking the question philosophers and sages have pondered throughout time: "What is truth?" And we sense the tragic mistake Pilate made as he left the room before he had a chance to hear the Savior's answer.

We see Jesus affirming before Pilate that He truly is a king, though His kingdom is not of this world.

We see the incredible hypocrisy shown by the scribes and Pharisees, who would commit murder using all the legal tricks at their disposal, but who refused to enter Pilate's palace for fear they would be "defiled" before the Passover.

Perhaps most of all, we see the shame and the pain that our Savior bore. The shame and the pain that we by our sins have deserved.

As you teach this lesson, pray that the Holy Spirit would work a new and fuller awareness of Jesus' love in the hearts of each student. Pray for the ability to communicate clearly and completely the truth of that love as God the Holy Spirit impresses it on the hearts of your students today.

GETTING INTO THE LESSON (Objectives 1 and 4)

The Student Book describes the debate you will conduct during this class period. Divide the students in your class into two groups as described in their books. You will want to plan this division carefully so as to have the group divided as evenly as possible. Take into account both students' Bible knowledge and their verbal ability.

Remind students to read both sets of arguments because they will need to answer their opponents' challenges. Encourage them to look back at the Passion accounts from Matthew, Mark, and Luke as well as the account in John.

Give each group help as they need it, but let them work out the details on their own as much as possible.

Allow about 20 minutes for the debate itself. Referee and make sure that each student has an opportunity to contribute. After the debate is over, reserve some time to evaluate what the students discovered. Ask their feelings and opinions at this point about Jesus' trial.

If no one mentions it, point out that the side "For the Prosecution"

had a big disadvantage: Jesus was innocent! He did not deserve to die!

FOR FURTHER THOUGHT (Objectives 2, 3, and 4)

These questions have been designed to summarize some of the other main ideas from the pericope the students read today. Discuss these as time permits. Consider assigning some of them for completion in writing outside of class.

Reading assignment for next time: John 20:19-31

Session 42: Are You Sure?

BIBLE BASIS: John 20

CENTRAL TRUTH

Jesus truly lives. When we experience doubt and fear, His Spirit helps us conquer all our doubts and uncertainties. We have not yet seen, but by His grace we can believe.

OBJECTIVES

That the students will:
1. Describe Thomas' doubts and the reasons that lay behind them
2. Identify the doubts in their own hearts and confess these as sin
3. Use the word study method to explore the meaning of "doubt" and practice this form of in-depth Bible study
4. Share their doubts and fears with other Christians when they find themselves in need of strength and the assurance of God's forgiveness

BACKGROUND

What is faith? How would you define this word or explain it, to a 6- or 8-year-old child, for example?

The world often ridicules the Christian faith. But the kind of faith the world often means is not Biblical faith but unexamined, mindless faith. We all know Christians who have never examined their beliefs, who have never grown in knowledge or personal application much beyond what they learned in confirmation instruction. Such people certainly may have saving faith. Yet they are missing much of what God the Holy Spirit would like to give them. The Scripture contains some stinging words written to a group of believers with "faith" like that in **Heb. 5:11-14**.

At the other extreme, we find Christians whose doubts and questions continually undermine their trust in the Lord Jesus. They insist on seeing before they will believe. For them, the facts they apprehend with their senses are more real than the truth written in God's Word. This too is sin. In many--and perhaps most--cases, these kinds of doubts spring from personal pride.

Thomas refused to believe that Jesus had risen. As Jesus had made clear on other occasions, such unbelief is an act of the human will. Thomas himself said, **"Unless I see . . . I will not believe."** (Compare **John 7:16-18**.) Sinners do not want to believe. We rebel at the thought of bringing our thoughts captive to the obedience of Christ **(2 Cor. 10:5.)**

Then, too, perhaps Thomas' doubts arose from his own sense of guilt. Certainly Thomas recognized both his own cowardice and that of the other disciples. If Jesus really had come back to life, what would He say to them? think of them? How could they respond to His questions about their loyalty in light of their defection at the very time He needed them most?

How good it is to know that, no matter what reasons lie behind our doubt, God forgives. His Spirit keeps us in faith and strengthens our faith.

The students in your class have probably begun, or will soon begin, what will for at least some be a difficult task--that of making their faith their own. Up to the time of early adolescence, most children accept the statements of their pastor, parents, and teachers without question, especially when these authority figures speak about God and matters of faith.

But beginning in the junior high years and continuing on through high school, young people reexamine their beliefs. Their cognitive abilities expand to enable them to think abstractly in a way never before possible. Adolescence and doubts often go hand in hand.

As you teach today, stress the idea that we can ask God to explain His Word and His work to us. He won't become angry. Rather, He will help us find answers to our questions. It's not wrong to ask sincere questions and to wonder about what God is like and how He acts.

But point out that all Christians experience sinful doubt at times. We all fail to trust God. We all accuse Him and rebel against what His Word plainly tells us. At these times, He continues to love us. He draws us back to Himself, enables us to repent, and assures us of His forgiveness and of His strength in our own weakness.

Pray that your students will receive an increased awareness of the immensity of His grace and goodness as they study today's lesson.

GETTING INTO THE LESSON (Objective 2)

Ask students to fill out the "faith inventory" on the first page of their books. Assure them that they need not share their answers aloud unless they choose to do so. You will return to this part of the lesson later on, so don't spend too much time discussing it now.

DOUBTING THOMAS (Objective 1)

Use this exercise to help the class put themselves "into Thomas's sandals." What would they have felt and thought? After students have had a chance to write, share paragraphs.

DOUBT, FEAR, AND FAILURE (Objectives 2 and 3)

This section of the lesson will involve students in a word study to increase their awareness of God's attitude toward doubt and His prescription for dealing with it. In addition to what they will learn about the topic itself, they will in essence review a Bible study technique they have used several times during this course. By this time, they should be familiar with the procedure. Have students work in groups of two or three. Help individuals or groups as they need it. Note that they are to record their results in their notebooks.

Be sure to allow time for comparing notes after the word study has been completed.

FAITH VS. DOUBT (Objectives 2 and 4)

Affirm the idea that all Christians experience doubt at times. Discuss the difference between sincerely wanting to know God's will and His character as opposed to doubting His goodness or His truthfulness.

Examine the various reasons given for doubt listed in the Student Book. Discuss them briefly. Then go back to the statements students marked at the beginning of the lesson period. What reasons lie behind many of our doubts?

THOMAS AND ME (Objective 4)

Use this final section of the lesson to emphasize the wonderful news of God's grace. Assure students that God will help us with our questions and will forgive us for our doubts.

Affirm the thought that sometimes it helps to share our concerns with other Christians. Often they can answer our doubts. Always they can pray with us and for us, and they can assure us of God's forgiveness and love.

Reading assignment for next time: John 21

Session 43: Feed My Lambs

BIBLE BASIS: John 21

CENTRAL TRUTH

Jesus calls us to faith and gives us a mission and purpose for living. He forgives our faithlessness and empowers us to follow Him in the ministry to which He calls us.

OBJECTIVES

That the students will:
1. Analyze the growing and

maturing process Peter experienced as a disciple of Jesus

    2. Think about the growth and maturation God is working in their own lives right now and thank Him for it

    3. Ask God to direct their future career choices so that they might use their entire lives to glorify Him and to build the Kingdom

    4. Consider the options available for full-time professional ministry in Jesus' kingdom

BACKGROUND

From the beginning, Jesus had chosen Peter to serve His people in a unique way. Peter experienced several agonizing crises of commitment as he grew in his relationship with the Lord. Yet the Holy Spirit sustained him in each as the Savior forgave his faithlessness and drew the disciple back to Himself.

Peter was both humbled and refined through his experiences as he little by little became the "rock"--the mature, stable pillar Jesus knew he would someday become.

Still today, most young believers recapitulate Peter's patterns of growth. At times, young Christians boldly confess their Lord. At other times, they fall flat on their faces, giving in to seemingly meager temptations. During today's session, you can share with them the Good News that God will not give up on them. He will continue to help them grow. He will forgive them when they fail and will stand beside them each time they experience victory. One day, by God's grace, they will find themselves the mature, consistent disciples they long to be.

What a wonder it is that Jesus chooses to use people, weak though they are, to share the Gospel. He could have used angels to share the Gospel, but instead He chose to use Peter, Thomas, and the other disciples. Today He gives us the great privilege of "feeding His lambs and sheep."

As you plan for today's lesson, you may want to write to the Board for Professional Education Services of The Lutheran Church--Missouri Synod, 1333 S. Kirkwood Road, St. Louis, Missouri 63122-7295. This board produces materials encouraging young people to consider full-time professional ministry in the church as they make career choices. Or get materials from a nearby Lutheran college. Think too about your potential in encouraging students to think along these lines. Your personal witness could be one of the most effective recruitment tools the Holy Spirit will use in the life of one or more young people in your class.

GETTING INTO THE LESSON (Objective 2)

Discuss the question from the Student Book about the phrase, "Grow up!" Ask the class what people mean when they use this expression.

Then read the two passages from Peter's epistles. These verses both talk about growing as Christians. You will return to these verses a little later in the period, so you need not exhaust their meaning at this point.

GROWING PAINS (Objectives 1 and 2)

Have the students work through the first activity in this section on their own. Give individuals help as needed. Answers may vary somewhat, but it should be fairly obvious that at times in Peter's life, he stood strong in faith. At other times, he wavered and failed miserably. At still other times, he seemed to grow through rather painful experiences. Discuss the students' answers and the reasons they responded as they did.

The last paragraph in this section asks students about the peaks and valleys in every Christian's life. Bring out the fact that all of us experience times of strength and times of weakness. As you talk about specific times of strength and weakness in your own life and in the lives of your students, assure the students that Jesus understands the growing process even better than we do. (Sometimes we don't even understand ourselves!) But Jesus always forgives our weakness and failures and continues to offer us His strength.

Also point out that Christians grow in faith as they use the Word and the Sacraments. As we grow, we become more consistent in our response to difficult circumstances. Even though mature Christians still sin, we can grow and mature in faith. Then we will be more stable and experience more and more victory in our Christian life.

You will certainly also want to assure students that God does not love "mature" Christians any more than He loves "immature" ones. We are all justified in the same way--by God's grace through faith in Jesus.

Return to the passages from Peter's epistles at this point. Note the characteristics Peter says will become more evident in our lives as we "grow in grace."

WILL I EVER GROW UP? (Objective 3)

Tell the students that this letter was written by a 9th grade student to his religion teacher. Ask the students how they would answer his letter. The Student Book allows space for them to list five main points. Let each student work to complete the list independently. Then discuss their lists.

Depending on the level of trust your students feel toward one another (and toward you), you may be able to discuss similar frustration they feel at not being able to conquer their own immaturity. As you minister to these kinds of concerns, continue to repeat the assurance that God always forgives us even for sins we commit "knowing better." Also assure them that the Holy Spirit wants to work in their lives and will continue to help them "grow up" in their faith. However, the Spirit does not float through the air like some heavenly electricity. He uses means--His Word, the Lord's Supper, and Baptism. Talk together about ways their faith is strengthened through these means of grace. Encourage them to draw upon the Spirit's power as they face difficult situations in their lives.

CHOSEN AND CALLED TO SERVE
(Objective 4)

This final section is meant to interest students in learning more about full-time professional ministry in the church. Use any information you have gotten from the Board for Professional Education Services or a college. Also encourage students to interview one or more professional church workers. Students should find out what this person does day by day in his or her work and how that person feels about the ministry in which he or she is engaged.

Guide interested students to other resources for more information about the particular vocation(s) in which they are interested.

Session 44: Fly Like an Eagle

BIBLE BASIS: John 1--2

CENTRAL TRUTH

John wrote his gospel under the inspiration of the Holy Spirit so that we might believe that Jesus is the Son of God and that we might receive eternal life through faith in Him. In this gospel, God has given the world a unique and powerful insight into His plan of salvation through Jesus.

OBJECTIVES

That the students will:
1. Summarize the major terms and doctrinal themes they have learned throughout their study of John's gospel
2. Describe the major persons with whom Jesus interacted during His earthly ministry as recorded by John
3. Restate the commonly accepted key verse of John's gospel (20:31) and defend the choice of this verse as the key verse
4. Find the "I Am" statements Jesus made as recorded by John and be able to tell what each means for their personal lives

BACKGROUND

You will use this session to review the major themes and characters from John's gospel in preparation for the evaluation activity to be given during session 45. You may want to spend at least part of today's lesson period looking back over John's gospel,

79

chapter by chapter. Encourage students to comment on what they remember from each chapter and to restate the central truths of each section of the gospel in their own words.

GETTING INTO THE LESSON (Objectives 1, 2, 3, and 4)

Have students look through this lesson in their books. Tell them they will use today's class period to work through these review activities, recording their responses in their notebooks as the Student Book directs.

You may want to allow students who wish to work with a partner. Make yourself available to answer any questions students may have.

Remind the class that you will collect notebooks during the class period next time to evaluate them.

Session 45: Concluding Activities

BIBLE BASIS: The Book of John

The material that follows suggests one possible way to evaluate what the students learned and retained during this course. You may or may not wish to administer a written test to your class. If you find a better way to evaluate the students' progress, by all means use it. Not all teaching situations call for a written examination. The material here is optional and may be adapted for use. Your particular instructional circumstances will determine when and how you can best evaluate.

In the same way, your teaching style and Scriptural emphases may vary from that of other teachers in other classrooms and from year to year within the same school. Therefore if you decide to give a written test, it will be unique to a certain extent. Use the questions suggested below as a resource when you write your own test. Be sure to include questions aimed at evaluating student knowledge, understanding, and practical application of Biblical truth to daily life.

You may want to allow students to use their notebooks as they take the test. This will reward students who have done a good job in keeping their notebooks. In any case, you should check the student notebooks as a part of your total evaluation of student work during this unit and throughout the quarter.

MATCHING QUESTIONS

Match the people listed below with the descriptions or quotations that follow.

(C) Thomas
(J) Abraham
(A) Lazarus
(F) Judas
(D) Nicodemus
(B) Caiaphas
(I) Peter
(G) John the Baptizer
(E) Pontius Pilate
(H) Pharisee

A. arose from the dead
B. high priest
C. "I'll believe it when I see it!"
D. "How can I be born again?"
E. condemned Jesus to death by crucifixion
F. betrayed Jesus with a kiss
G. announced the coming of the promised Messiah
H. an expert in religious law
I. was told, "Feed My lambs"
J. father of the Jewish nation
K. the Anointed One of God

SHORT ANSWER

1. List as many "I am" statements of Jesus from John's gospel. Choose one and tell what it means to your life as a teenager today.
2. Explain the difference between a gospel and the Gospel.
3. Jesus spoke often about His hour of glory. What was that hour of glory? Why did He call it that?
4. According to John the author, why did he write his gospel account?
5. Suppose an unbeliever asked you, "What does it mean to be born again? How can a person be born of

water and the Spirit? What good would that be?" How would you answer these questions?

6. Explain the difference between Law and Gospel. Include what each is and what each does.

7. Why does John refer to Jesus' miracles as signs?

8. Jesus is given each of these titles in John's gospel. Explain what each means.
   a. Messiah:
   b. Logos:
   c. Good Shepherd:
   d. Rabbi:

9. Jesus referred to the cup the Father had given Him that He was about to drink. Tell what Jesus meant by this cup. Why did He have to drink it? What difference does the fact that He did drink this cup make in your life?

ESSAY QUESTION

You have been studying John's gospel for a number of weeks now. Choose one memory verse you learned that is especially significant to you. It may be comforting to you, challenging to you, or exciting to you. Write the verse here and tell why you chose that particular verse.

(**Note to teachers:** If you did not assign passages for memory work during this course, ask the students to recall instead a specific concept or idea from the gospel that was comforting, challenging, or exciting to them. They should describe what this was and then tell why they chose this particular concept as particularly significant to them personally.)

Feel free to duplicate the above questions for use in testing. Please add the following credit line: Concordia Publishing House, copyright 1986. Used by permission.

Bibliography

Blaiklock, E. M., editor. *The Zondervan Pictorial Bible Atlas*. Grand Rapids: Zondervan, 1972.

Comparative Study of Bible Translations and Paraphrases. St. Louis: Commission on Theology and Church Relations, The Lutheran Church--Missouri Synod, 1975.

Halley, Henry H. *Halley's Bible Handbook*. Grand Rapids: Zondervan, 1976.

Hummel, Horace. *The Word Becoming Flesh*. St. Louis: Concordia, 1979.

Kretzmann, Paul E. *Popular Commentary of the Bible* (vol. 1: The Old Testament). St. Louis: Concordia, 1923.

Lenski, R. C. H. *The Interpretation of John's Gospel*. Columbus: Lutheran Book Concern, 1931.

Morris, Leon. *Gospel of John*. Grand Rapids: Eerdmans, 1970.

Roehrs, Walter and Martin H. Franzmann. *The Concordia Self-Study Commentary*. St. Louis: Concordia, 1979.

Tenney, Merrill C., ed. *The Zondervan Pictorial Bible Dictionary*. Grand Rapids: Zondervan, 1967.

Wharton, Gary. *The New Compact Topical Bible*. Grand Rapids: Zondervan, 1972.

www.ingramcontent.com/pod-product-compliance
Lightning Source LLC
Chambersburg PA
CBHW080349170426
43194CB00014B/2734